First World War
and Army of Occupation
War Diary
France, Belgium and Germany

47 DIVISION
Divisional Troops
Royal Army Veterinary Corps
47 Mobile Veterinary Section
1 September 1915 - 9 May 1919

WO95/2726/1

The Naval & Military Press Ltd
www.nmarchive.com
Published in association with The National Archives

Published by

The Naval & Military Press Ltd

Unit 10 Ridgewood Industrial Park,

Uckfield, East Sussex,

TN22 5QE England

Tel: +44 (0) 1825 749494

www.naval-military-press.com

www.nmarchive.com

This diary has been reprinted in facsimile from the original. Any imperfections are inevitably reproduced and the quality may fall short of modern type and cartographic standards.

© Crown Copyright
Images reproduced by permission of The National Archives, London, England, 2015.

Contents

Document type	Place/Title	Date From	Date To
Heading	WO95/2726/1 47 Division 47 Mobile Vetinary Section Sept 1915-Mar 1919		
Heading	47th Division 47th Mobile Vety Section Sep 1915-Mar 1919		
Heading	47th Division 47th Mobile Vety Section Vol I Sept 15		
War Diary	Gosnay	01/09/1915	01/09/1915
War Diary	Brvay	02/09/1915	26/09/1915
War Diary	Drouvin	27/09/1915	28/09/1915
War Diary	Neoux Les Mines	29/09/1915	30/09/1915
Heading	47th Division 47th Mobile Vety Section Vol II Oct 15		
Heading	War Diary Of Mobile Veterinary Section 47 London Division From Oct 1 1915 To Oct 31 1915 Volume II		
War Diary	Hesdigneul	01/10/1915	05/10/1915
War Diary	Bruay	06/10/1915	10/10/1915
War Diary	Noeux Les Mines	11/10/1915	14/10/1915
War Diary	Bruay to Noeux Les Mines	15/10/1915	15/10/1915
War Diary	Noeux Les Mines	16/10/1915	31/10/1915
Heading	47th Division 1/2 London Mob. Vet. Sec. Nov Vol III		
Heading	War Diary Of Mobile Veterinary Section 47th London Div. From 1.11.15 To 30.11.15		
War Diary	Noeux Les Mines	01/11/1915	14/11/1915
War Diary	Mensecq	15/11/1915	30/11/1915
Heading	War Diary Of 1/2 Mobile Veterinary Section 47 (London) Div From 1-12-15 To 31-12-15 Vol IV		
War Diary	Mensecq	01/12/1915	14/12/1915
War Diary	Drouvin	15/12/1915	31/12/1915
Heading	47th Div 1/2 London Mobl. Vety Section Jan Vol V		
War Diary	Drouvin	01/01/1916	31/01/1916
Heading	War Diary Of 1/2 London Mobile Vet. Section From Feb 1 1916 To Feb 29 1916		
War Diary	Drouvin	01/02/1916	15/02/1916
War Diary	Lillers	16/02/1916	29/02/1916
Heading	War Diary Of 1/2 London Mobile Vet. Section Vol VII From 1.3.16 To 31.3.16		
War Diary	Lillers	01/03/1916	08/03/1916
War Diary	Bruay	09/03/1916	15/03/1916
War Diary	Caucourt	16/03/1916	21/03/1916
War Diary	Heripre	22/03/1916	27/03/1916
War Diary	Fresnicourt	28/03/1916	31/03/1916
Heading	War Diary Of 1/2 London Mobile Vet. Section 47th London Div From 1-4-16 To 30-4-16 Vol VIII		
War Diary	Fresnicourt	01/04/1916	30/04/1916
Miscellaneous	War Diary Mobile Veterinary Section 47th London Div From 1.5.16 To 31.5.16 Vol 9		
War Diary	Fresnicourt	01/05/1916	26/05/1916
War Diary	Bruay	27/05/1916	31/05/1916
Miscellaneous	47th Division	05/08/1916	05/08/1916
Miscellaneous	To H.Q. 47th London Div.	04/08/1916	04/08/1916
Heading	War Diary Of 1/2 London Mobile Vet. Section From 1.7.1916 To 31.7.1916. Vol XI		

War Diary	Barlin	01/07/1916	18/07/1916
War Diary	Fresnicourt	19/07/1916	27/07/1916
War Diary	La Theoloye	28/07/1916	31/07/1916
Heading	War Diary Of 1/2 London Mobile Veterinary Section 47th London Div. From 1.8.16 To 31.8.16. Vol 12		
War Diary	Frohen Le Grand	01/08/1916	03/08/1916
War Diary	Yvrench	04/08/1916	15/08/1916
War Diary	Neuf Moulin	16/08/1916	22/08/1916
War Diary	Baizieux	23/08/1916	31/08/1916
Miscellaneous	To H.Q. 47th London Div.		
Heading	War Diary Of 1/2 London Mobile Veterinary Section 47th London Div. From 1.9.16 To 30.9.16 Vol 13		
War Diary	Baizieux	01/09/1916	11/09/1916
War Diary	Albert	12/09/1916	30/09/1916
Miscellaneous	To A.D.V.S. 47th London Div.	05/11/1916	05/11/1916
Heading	War Diary Of 1/2 London Mobile Vet. Section 47th London Div. From 1.10.16 To 31.10.16 Vol 14		
War Diary	Albert	01/10/1916	05/10/1916
War Diary	Fricourt	06/10/1916	10/10/1916
War Diary	Baizieux	11/10/1916	12/10/1916
War Diary	St Sauvier	13/10/1916	13/10/1916
War Diary	Eaucourt	14/10/1916	18/10/1916
War Diary	Sheet.27. L.29.a.7.4	19/10/1916	31/10/1916
Miscellaneous	To H.Q 47th London Div.	05/12/1916	05/12/1916
Heading	War Diary Of 1/2 London Mobile Veterinary Section From 1.11.16 To 30.11.1916 Vol 15		
War Diary	Sheet 27 L.29.d.7.5	01/11/1917	30/11/1917
Miscellaneous	To H.Q 47th London Div.	05/01/1917	05/01/1917
Heading	War Diary Of 1/2 London Mobile Veterinary Section 47th London Div. From 1.12.16 To 31.12.16 Vol 16		
War Diary	Sheet 27 L.29.d.7.4	01/12/1917	31/12/1917
Miscellaneous	To H.Q 47th London Div.	04/02/1917	04/02/1917
Heading	War Diary Of 1/2 London Mobile Veterinary Section 47th London Div. From 1.1.17 To 31.1.17 Vol 17		
War Diary	Sheet 27 L.29.d.7.4	01/01/1917	31/01/1917
Heading	War Diary Of 1/2 London Mobile Veterinary Section From 1.2.1917 To 28.2.1917 Vol 18		
War Diary	Sheet 27 L.29.d.7.5	01/02/1917	28/02/1917
Heading	War Diary Of 1/2 London Mobile Veterinary Section From 1.3.17 To 31.3.17 Vol 19		
War Diary	Sheet 27 L.29.d.7.4	01/03/1917	31/03/1917
Heading	War Diary Of 1/2 London Mobile Veterinary Section 47th London Div. From 1.4.17 To 30.4.17 Vol 20		
War Diary	Sheet 27 L.29.d.7.5	01/04/1917	30/04/1917
Heading	War Diary Of 1/2 London Mobile Veterinary Section From 1.5.17 To 31.5.17 Vol 21		
War Diary	Sheet 27 L.29.d.7.4	01/05/1917	26/05/1917
War Diary	Sheet 28 G.34.b.8.10	27/05/1917	31/05/1917
Heading	War Diary Of 1/2 London Mobile Veterinary Section From 1.6.17 To 30.6.17 Vol 22		
War Diary	Sheet 28 G.34.b.8.10	01/06/1917	13/06/1917
War Diary	G.32.d.8.1	14/06/1917	30/06/1917
Heading	War Diary Of 1/2 London Mobile Veterinary Section 47th (London) Div. From 1.7.17 To 31.7.17 Vol 23		
War Diary	Sheet 28 N.7.a.8.5	01/07/1917	22/07/1917
War Diary	G.32.d.9.0	22/07/1916	31/07/1916

Heading	War Diary Of 1/2 London Mobile Veterinary Section 47th London Div. From 1.8.17 To 31.8.17 Vol 24		
War Diary	Sheet 28 G.32.a.9.0	01/08/1916	14/08/1916
War Diary	Wizernes	15/08/1917	21/08/1917
War Diary	Laleulene	22/08/1917	24/08/1917
War Diary	Sheet 29 H.13.d.9.3	25/08/1917	31/08/1917
Heading	War Diary Of 1/2 London Mobile Veterinary Section From 1.9.17 To 30.9.17 Vol 25		
War Diary	Sheet 28 H.13.d.9.3	01/09/1917	04/09/1917
War Diary	Sheet 28 G.22.d.2.4	05/09/1917	18/09/1917
War Diary	Godewaersvelde	19/09/1917	21/09/1917
War Diary	Lens 11 Savy Berlette	22/09/1917	22/09/1917
War Diary	Maroeuil	23/09/1917	25/09/1917
War Diary	Sheet 51B G.1.d.8.1	26/09/1917	30/09/1917
Heading	War Diary Of 1/2 London Mobile Veterinary Section From 1.10.17 To 31.10.17 Vol 26		
War Diary	G.1.d.8.1	01/10/1917	08/10/1917
War Diary	Sheet 51c. G.1.d.8.1	09/10/1917	12/10/1917
War Diary	Sheet 51B G.1.d.8.1	13/10/1917	31/10/1917
Heading	War Diary Of 1/2 London Mobile Veterinary Section From 1/11/17 To 30/11/17 Vol 27		
War Diary	Sheet 28 G.1.8.1	01/11/1917	22/11/1917
War Diary	Lens 11 Dainville	23/11/1917	23/11/1917
War Diary	Monchiet	24/11/1917	24/11/1917
War Diary	Sheet Lens 11 Achiet Le Petit	25/11/1917	27/11/1917
War Diary	Bapaume	28/11/1917	28/11/1917
War Diary	Sheet 57c N 4 B Central	29/11/1917	30/11/1917
War Diary	Bapaume	01/12/1917	03/12/1917
War Diary	Neuville	04/12/1917	16/12/1917
War Diary	Bus	17/12/1917	28/02/1918
Miscellaneous	To D.A.D.V.S. 47 London Div.	04/04/1918	04/04/1918
Heading	War Diary Of 1/2 London Mobile Veterinary Section From 1/3/18 To 31/3/18 Vol 31		
War Diary	Sheet 57c O.24.C.	01/03/1918	23/03/1918
War Diary	Guillemont	24/03/1918	24/03/1918
War Diary	Dernancourt	25/03/1918	25/03/1918
War Diary	Warloy	26/03/1918	26/03/1918
War Diary	Vauchelles	27/03/1918	27/03/1918
War Diary	Lens 11 Map Puchevillers	28/03/1918	29/03/1918
War Diary	Septenville	30/03/1918	31/03/1918
War Diary	Septenville	01/04/1918	09/04/1918
War Diary	Nal De Maison	10/04/1918	13/04/1918
War Diary	Domvast	14/04/1918	29/04/1918
War Diary	Brucamps	30/04/1918	30/04/1918
Heading	War Diary Of 1/2nd London Mobile Vety Section From 1/5/18 To 31/5/18 Vol 33		
War Diary	Allonville	01/05/1918	01/05/1918
War Diary	Beaucourt	02/05/1918	31/05/1918
Heading	War Diary Of 1/2 London Mobile Veterinary Section From June 1st 1918 To June 30th 1918 Vol 34		
War Diary	Beaucourt	01/06/1918	02/06/1918
War Diary	T.29.a.82.57.d	03/06/1918	17/06/1918
War Diary	Sheet 57d T.29.a.8.2.	18/06/1918	20/06/1918
War Diary	Breilly	21/06/1918	12/07/1918
War Diary	Montigny	13/07/1918	31/07/1918

Heading	War Diary Of 1/2 London Mobile Veterinary Section From 1.8.18 To 31.8.18		
War Diary	Montigny	01/08/1918	11/08/1918
War Diary	St Gratien	12/08/1918	13/08/1918
War Diary	Bonnay	14/08/1918	26/08/1918
War Diary	Mericourt	27/08/1918	28/08/1918
War Diary	Meaulte	29/08/1918	30/08/1918
War Diary	Map 62d F.4.c	31/08/1918	31/08/1918
Heading	War Diary Of 1/2 London Mobile Veterinary Section From 1-9-18 To 30-9-18 Vol 38		
War Diary	Mametz	01/09/1918	04/09/1918
War Diary	Hardicourt	05/09/1918	06/09/1918
War Diary	Corbie	07/09/1918	08/09/1918
War Diary	Heilly	09/09/1918	13/09/1918
War Diary	Lapugnoy	14/09/1918	26/09/1918
War Diary	Hernicourt	27/09/1918	30/09/1918
Miscellaneous	To D.A.D.V.S 47th Divn	01/11/1918	01/11/1918
Heading	War Diary Of 1/2 London Mobile Veterinary Section From October 1st 1918 To October 31st 1918		
War Diary	Nedon	01/10/1918	01/10/1918
War Diary	Lestrum	02/10/1918	04/10/1918
War Diary	Pont Duhem	05/10/1918	17/10/1918
War Diary	Mazinghem	18/10/1918	24/10/1918
War Diary	Estaires	25/10/1918	25/10/1918
War Diary	Lomme	26/10/1918	27/10/1918
War Diary	Fives-Lille	28/10/1918	31/10/1918
War Diary	Willems	01/11/1918	13/11/1918
War Diary	Froyennes	14/11/1918	16/11/1918
War Diary	Chereng	17/11/1918	30/11/1918
War Diary	Map 5A Ferfay	01/12/1918	05/12/1918
War Diary	Map 44B E.7.c.2.7	06/12/1918	31/01/1919
War Diary	Labeuvriere	01/02/1919	28/02/1919
War Diary	Lozinghem	01/03/1919	31/03/1919
War Diary	Camblain Chatelain	01/05/1919	09/05/1919

WO 95/2736/1

47 DIVISION

47 MOBILE VETINARY SECTION
SEPT 1915 - MAR 1919

47TH DIVISION

47TH MOBILE VETY SECTION

SEP 1915 – MAR 1919

121/7016

47th Division

47th Mobile Vety Section

Vol I.
Sept 15

Sep '15 -
Mar '19

WAR DIARY or INTELLIGENCE SUMMARY.

(Erase heading not required.)

Army Form C. 2118.

Instructions regarding War Diaries and Intelligence Summaries are contained in F.S. Regs., Part II. and the Staff Manual respectively. Title pages will be prepared in manuscript.

Hour, Date, Place	Summary of Events and Information	Remarks and references to Appendices
Sept 1st 1915 Germay	Twenty three horses evacuated from Chocques station to the No 5 Veterinary Hospital. First pass by ADVS which was then issued to mens Sester to Bandet & Australophtoday done in evening.	
Sept 2nd 1915 Sunday	Visit from Capt Lumgenjet as DAAQMG. the ADVS. Notes the train and enspects horse lines for hour removed from Allenagne which let him left Pekmy 4g 22 refelut of N.M. Regt. Asparty with puria (resend) as reinforcements for Avoir (pencil) Mahey (pencil) Mr K's camp advents.	
Sept 3rd 1915 Friday	4 horses flesh from Bois de Namis and shate two Mines Horses (C. Squadron REH HeeD DAAQMG with regard to circumstances Meyors Shippard further finds and other frames foru form ADS. Stores arrives for ADVS at DROUVIN	

WAR DIARY
or
INTELLIGENCE SUMMARY.
(Erase heading not required.)

Army Form C. 2118.

Instructions regarding War Diaries and Intelligence Summaries are contained in F.S. Regs., Part II. and the Staff Manual respectively. Title pages will be prepared in manuscript.

Hour, Date, Place	Summary of Events and Information	Remarks and references to Appendices
Sept 4th 1915 Bomar	Pte Sheppard evacuated to base hospital. Inspected Divisional Train and asked Visited Divisional Headquarters and from thence went to Divisional Station to examine HR & on Remounts. One Remount sent to M.V.S.	J.S
Sept 5th 1915 Bomar	Went to A.D.V.S. (riding) declaration of the H horses (geldings) on the 3rd instant. Visited A.S.C. and saw all sick cases. Section Routine.	J.S
Sept 6th 1915 Bomar	Saw Lorry Autofrap. Details of (Arames). Asking Water Allowance. Asked Headquarters and asked for instructions to do press of & supplies Inspecte and Remounts. Visit A.S.C. and Officers to discuss matters. See to Horses and Cognitive letters to Serve. Horses sick horses attended	J.S

Army Form C. 2118.

WAR DIARY
or
INTELLIGENCE SUMMARY.
(Erase heading not required.)

Instructions regarding War Diaries and Intelligence Summaries are contained in F.S. Regs., Part II. and the Staff Manual respectively. Title pages will be prepared in manuscript.

Hour, Date, Place	Summary of Events and Information	Remarks and references to Appendices
Sept 7th 1915 BRUAY	Attached all Companies ASC. 17 Cars attached. 1 Car sent to duty. ADYS visited everton in the evening (Visited) K.E.H. and H.Q. Headquarters. Season Routine.	
Sept 8 1915 BRUAY	DDYS and ADYS (both) Litter in morning 10 horse admitted. Sicker Routine.	
Sept 9 1915 BRUAY	36 horses evacuated to No 5 horse Vet. hospital. 6 horses admitted, 2 destroyed, 1 died, 2 sent to duty.	
Sept 10th 1915 BRUAY	DDYS and ADYS made letter at Midday. 2 letters admitted. Visited ASC workshop, Artiste, and Office on return in evening. Season Routine.	

Army Form C. 2118.

WAR DIARY
or
INTELLIGENCE SUMMARY.
(Erase heading not required.)

Instructions regarding War Diaries and Intelligence Summaries are contained in F. S. Regs., Part II. and the Staff Manual respectively. Title pages will be prepared in manuscript.

Hour, Date, Place	Summary of Events and Information	Remarks and references to Appendices
Sept 11th 1915 BRAY	A.D.V.S. visits Section. 3 horses admitted sick. 3 horses sent to duty and one destroyed. Work Received from Section. Routine.	
Sept 12-1915 BRAY	Three horses admitted sick. 2 horses were cast and preparations started for the formation of the Brames Moving Station.	O.C.
Sept 13th 1915 BRAY	A.D.V.S. visits Section. 11 horses admitted. Visited Receival from H.P. Section Routine.	
Sept 14th 1915 BRAY	M. Cleanach's interpreter to the section ordered to proceed to Noeux les Mines to take over duties with the APM. 5 horses admitted. Sent to duty. Section Routine.	

Forms/C. 2118/10

Army Form C. 2118.

WAR DIARY
or
INTELLIGENCE SUMMARY.
(Erase heading not required.)

Instructions regarding War Diaries and Intelligence Summaries are contained in F.S. Regs., Part II. and the Staff Manual respectively. Title pages will be prepared in manuscript.

Hour, Date, Place	Summary of Events and Information	Remarks and references to Appendices
Sept 15th 1915 BRUAY	32 horses sent to No 5 Base Hospital 2 horses sent to duty. 10 F8 mules sicken. Pack mules and men	
Sept 16th 1915 BRUAY	6 horses admitted (Aubaye) 1 died Y.d.D. Removed (cavalry and Personnel of your empties) horses. Section Routine	
Sept 17 1915 BRUAY	2 horses (P. Smith) sick Return Received. horses OC ASC and elephant horses. Writes Section Routine	
Sept 18 1915 SAVAY	Six horses (P. Smith) one destroyed Received Return) Field OEE ADVS Route of proposal for change during the day	
Sept 19 1915 BRUAY	9 horses (P. Smith) (Aubaye) Returns Rendered Wires Lily for (change) Drawing Station OC n I Field of Murps Section Routine	

WAR DIARY
or
INTELLIGENCE SUMMARY.
(Erase heading not required.)

Army Form C. 2118.

Hour, Date, Place	Summary of Events and Information	Remarks and references to Appendices
Sept 20. 1915 BRAY	Stores admitted. 2 Anastasyes to duty. Identifyes Ordnance stores called (vide) A&QC graphite forms (vide) ask for Dressings Dressing Station. Met fuel arrangement for part of to come. Rest day	J.P.
Sept 21. 1915 BRAY	211 horses evacuated from Cheyne station to No 5 Base Vety Hospital. Dressing Post opened at Neuve-la-Ville (Orange) (Advance) Dressing post Station. Visited Orange Dressing Station to Fee Advance	J.P.
Sept 22. 1915 BRAY	Visit la Richie. to select a post for an Advance Dressing Post. Visited Advanced Dressing Station. Again, Rauken	J.P.
Sept 23. 1915 BRAY	Visited Advanced Collecting Station. Inspected horses at ASC at Senoncour Casualty. DDVS wires ceasing instructs to called a horse at Reserve Park. at to Albempre 3 at Albempre	J.P.

WAR DIARY
or
INTELLIGENCE SUMMARY.
(*Erase heading not required.*)

Army Form C. 2118.

Hour, Date, Place	Summary of Events and Information	Remarks and references to Appendices
Sept 24 1915 BRAY	Sought Roff and Wrych. Went to the 140th and 141st Infantry Brigade to perfect with 140th Brigade Headquarters the arrangements for the "Gatrack" to be used to M.V.S. to Corps Hd Qtrs. Advance Station was ADYS Poste (Harlan). Moved Station and returned Rouen	J.P.
Sept 25 1915 BRAY	Visited ADYS 9th Car Pst (Pouts) Ar Moeuvy arrived 37 Hours. 38th Hosp our ADVS Orders H.Q.	J.P.
Sept 26 1915 BRAY	Visited CCL instructed officer in charge to move to Mourse Chateau ADYS	J.P.
Sept 27 1915 DRUON	Went to Mourse Vist from ADVS Advance Moving Station before Rouen	J.P.

Army Form C. 2118.

WAR DIARY
or
INTELLIGENCE SUMMARY.
(Erase heading not required.)

Instructions regarding War Diaries and Intelligence Summaries are contained in F.S. Regs., Part II. and the Staff Manual respectively. Title pages will be prepared in manuscript.

Hour, Date, Place	Summary of Events and Information	Remarks and references to Appendices
Sept 28. 1915 Bruay	Orders to move from Bruay to the Nouex Branch. 25 horses from Nouex les Mines travels to Abbeville. Maj Buxton in evening.	
Sept 29th 1915 Nouex les Mines	A.D.V.S. visits. Section. Next to Bruay. Returns in afternoon. Great orders received to move section. Heavy rain for four days past. Have most been very muddy. Section routine.	
Sept 30th 1915 Nouex les Mines	Evacuated 15 horses from Nouex les mines Mines) sector to Headquarters in afternoon and pitched camp. Visit paid by A.D.V.S.	

Forms/C. 2118/10

121/7429

47th Division

47th Anti-tank Rty: Section

Oct 15

Army Form C. 2118.

WAR DIARY
or
INTELLIGENCE SUMMARY.
(Erase heading not required.)

Instructions regarding War Diaries and Intelligence Summaries are contained in F.S. Regs., Part II. and the Staff Manual respectively. Title pages will be prepared in manuscript.

Confidential.

War Diary

of

Mobile Veterinary Section.
47 London Division

from :-
Oct 1 1915

to :-
Oct 31. 1915.

Volume. V.

Original copy.

Army Form C. 2118.

WAR DIARY
or
INTELLIGENCE SUMMARY.
(Erase heading not required.)

Instructions regarding War Diaries and Intelligence Summaries are contained in F.S. Regs., Part II. and the Staff Manual respectively. Title pages will be prepared in manuscript.

Hour, Date, Place	Summary of Events and Information	Remarks and references to Appendices
October 1st 1915 HESDIGNEUL	Arranged camp. ADVS noted sector. (pre case discharged). Four cases admitted. Seven horses.	
October 2nd 1915 HESDIGNEUL	St Brown sent to No 2 Base Veterinary Hospital MARE. AFB122 sent to O.i/c AVS Remets at base. DDVS visited section, four cases admitted, one discharged. Four cases admitted, four horses.	
October 3rd 1915 HESDIGNEUL	ADVS visited section. (cases admitted) Return rendered. Seven horses.	
Oct 4th 1915 HESDIGNEUL	Sick horses evacuated from CHOCQUES. Fifteen cases admitted. Four Routine.	
October 5th 1915 HESDIGNEUL	Visited ADVS and AAQMG. Received orders to move the Mobile Section to BRUAY. the camp that we are temporarily located in having been made over (entirely) to Canadian cavalry Battalion. Scout peak Loaded to the Mayor.	

Forms/C. 2118/10

Army Form C. 2118.

WAR DIARY
or
INTELLIGENCE SUMMARY.
(Erase heading not required.)

Instructions regarding War Diaries and Intelligence Summaries are contained in F. S. Regs., Part II. and the Staff Manual respectively. Title pages will be prepared in manuscript.

Hour, Date, Place	Summary of Events and Information	Remarks and references to Appendices
October 6th 1915 BRUAY	Moved section piebald camp. ADVS visited section. Received orders to give veterinary assistance to ASC and King Edwards Horse.	JS
October 7th 1915 BRUAY	Visits ASC and King Edwards Horse. ADVS visits section. Conf (cleaner) orders to Bruay to rest day.	JS
October 8th 1915 BRUAY	Every two sick horses and one mule also one mule cast sent to Nos Rav Vety Hospital from CHOCQUES (foals) 15th (cavalry A/C) for Evacuation from No 2 Cav ASC	JS
October 9th 1915 BRUAY	N[o] sick. Owing to order veterinary ambulance too large for (I Troops) visited to ADVS to arrange for Horse (sick) all companies of New (section) Hors (sight) also R.E.H. and I Showcases Humanity (dairy) at bath parade for men. Visited DADOS	JS
October 10th 1915 BRUAY	section routine. (Sick) men. Blunt was one. Vet Rly returns. Visited Field Cavalry	JS

Forms/C. 2118/10
(9 29 6) W 4141—463 100,000 9/14 H W V

WAR DIARY
or
INTELLIGENCE SUMMARY.
(Erase heading not required.)

Army Form C. 2118.

Instructions regarding War Diaries and Intelligence Summaries are contained in F. S. Regs., Part II. and the Staff Manual respectively. Title pages will be prepared in manuscript.

Hour, Date, Place	Summary of Events and Information	Remarks and references to Appendices
Oct. 11th 1915. NOEUX LES MINES	Visited A.D.C. and advised on several veterinary matters. Visited 18 Hussars. Section Routine.	J.S.
Oct. 12th 1915. NOEUX LES MINES	Visited Divisional Train. A.V.S. visited M.V.S. Montmuit. How to select a suitable site for an advanced dressing station. The area was discussed and a place selected. A party was detailed and preparations made. Section Routine.	J.S.
Oct. 13th 1915 NOEUX LES MINES	Conducted party to advanced dressing station, which was opened on site selected the previous day — between Noeux le Mines and Mazingarbe. Evacuated 13 sick horses from Noeux les Mines Station. Visited Houchin. Saw a mule left behind by 19 Battalion. Visited Mine of Stonegreuil, which appears to be a deaw by me for damage done to the hedge by my horse.	J.S.
Oct. 14th 1915. NOEUX LES MINES	Visited A.D.C. and inspected horses. Collected mule from Houchin. Received notice to move in the morning.	J.S.

Forms/C. 2118/10

Army Form C. 2118.

WAR DIARY
or
INTELLIGENCE SUMMARY.
(Erase heading not required.)

Instructions regarding War Diaries and Intelligence Summaries are contained in F.S. Regs., Part II. and the Staff Manual respectively. Title pages will be prepared in manuscript.

Hour, Date, Place	Summary of Events and Information	Remarks and references to Appendices
Oct. 15th 1915. BRUAY & NOEUX LES MINES	Moved from Bruay to Noeux les Mines and pitched our Camp. Sick horses admitted. Section Routine.	JS
Oct. 16th 1915 NOEUX LES MINES	Twenty-two horses evacuated from Noeux les Mines station D.D.V.S.; O.C. Base Hospital, A.Dr.V.S. 47th Divn + 15th Bgd notified. Nine horses admitted.	JS
Oct 17th 1915. NEUX LES MINES	Section Routine, Visited R.C.O. and inspected horses. Went to Field Cashier and paid men. Went to horses and discovered a horse belonging to 7 R.F.A. which had been left behind by that unit. A Geiger Mfg. left with inhabitant. Three horses admitted.	JS
Oct 18th 1915. NOEUX LES MINES	Section Routine. Visited A.D.V.S. at Mesingarbe. Thirteen horses admitted. Arrangements made for evacuation.	JS
Oct 19th 1915 NOEUX LES MINES	Section Routine. Evacuated twenty two horses, including two cast by D.D.R. Visit from A.D.V.S. Inspected horses belonging to H.A.S.C. Visited transport lines of 4th London Field Amb.	JS

(9 29 6) W 4141—463 100,000 9/14 H W V   Forms/C. 2118/10

Army Form C. 2118.

WAR DIARY
or
INTELLIGENCE SUMMARY.
(Erase heading not required.)

Instructions regarding War Diaries and Intelligence Summaries are contained in F. S. Regs., Part II. and the Staff Manual respectively. Title pages will be prepared in manuscript.

Hour, Date, Place	Summary of Events and Information	Remarks and references to Appendices
Oct. 20. 1915 Noeux les MINES	ADMS visited M.V.S. Visited Divisional train attd or various veterinary points. DDVS paid a visit to M.V.S. Visited 1/5 Divisional Headquarters to arrange a point of area and to try and secure the present est. to the M.V.S. Visited Bruay and handed in the billeting certificates for that command.	JP
Oct 21. 1915 Noeux les MINES	Visited BOZINGHARBE. DDR. cast a section horse for sick. Section horses examined. Returned forwarded. Section eight horses cast close to. LIEUT. SOUTHALL went on leave to a	JP
October 22. 1915 Noeux les MINES		
Oct. 23rd 1915 NOEUX les MINES	O.D.V.S. visited section, and in company of Capt. Tweed inspected the remounts, also gave authority to dispose of mule found lay 1/2 R.E's north. Issued for 24 Horse rugs. Remitted 7	JP
Oct 24th 1915 NOEUX les MINES	A.D.V.S. visited section with Lieut. Craig and inspected all sick horses. Remitted 1, discharged 2.	JP
Oct 25th 1915 NEUXles MINES	Arrangements made for evacuation. Remitted 4.	JP
Oct 26. 1915 NEUX les MINES	A.D.V.S. visited section and afternoon which horses were Hucquemebs 2.6. Note sent asking for decision after of this horses. Two horses 15 U.Y. invalid killed and dressing N.C.O. to report in morning. Remitted 15. Two cases (colic) treated returned to duty.	JP

Forms/C. 2118/10

(9 29 6) W 4141—463 100,000 9/14 H W V

Army Form C. 2118.

WAR DIARY
or
INTELLIGENCE SUMMARY.
(Erase heading not required.)

Instructions regarding War Diaries and Intelligence Summaries are contained in F.S. Regs., Part II. and the Staff Manual respectively. Title pages will be prepared in manuscript.

Hour, Date, Place	Summary of Events and Information	Remarks and references to Appendices
Oct 27th 1915 NOEUX LES MINES	ADVS visited section. Loys Major visited Leigh. Admitted two discharged one. Road tests carried from entrance. Very wet weather. Rained all day long.	JP
October 28th 1915 Noeux les Mines	Very wet day. ADVS visited section in afternoon. Conducting party returned. Section routine.	JP
Oct 29th 1915 Noeux les Mines	DDVS and ADVS visited section. ADVS visited section in afternoon and inspected proposed camp. Mule lines by night guard through to 15th Div. 3 Remounts Brothers + sick. Stamps and Mullai received.	JP
Oct 30th 1915 Noeux les Mines	First Lowland returned from leave. Ayrs mules section. 9 cases admitted. Section routine.	JP
Oct 31 1915 Naux les MINES	ADVS visited section. Mules AS and KEH evacuated 13 sick cases and 2 egpt horses. Returned sent in sick men.	JP

1/2 London Mob. Vol. Soc. Vol III

12/
7655

CONFIDENTIAL.

War Diary
of
Mobile Veterinary Section
47th London Div.

From 1.110.16 to 30.11.16.

Army Form C. 2118.

WAR DIARY
INTELLIGENCE SUMMARY.
(Erase heading not required.) Mobile Veterinary Section
47 London Div.

Instructions regarding War Diaries and Intelligence Summaries are contained in F.S. Regs., Part II. and the Staff Manual respectively. Title pages will be prepared in manuscript.

Hour, Date, Place	Summary of Events and Information	Remarks and references to Appendices
Nov. 1. 1915. NOEUX LES MINES	A.D.V.S. visited Section. Six sick horses admitted, one picked sick immediately on arrival. Sixteen horses evacuated to R.E.H. ¼ A.S.C. lines.	J.S.
Nov. 2. 1915.	Seven sick horses admitted. Visited 707/? (Brig) R.F.A. (by request) and destroyed horse with fractured fetlock A.S.C. lines.	J.S.
Nov. 3. 1915.	A.D.V.S. visited Section. Fourteen sick horses evacuated to R.E. Hospital, twelve sick horses admitted. One mule destroyed.	J.S.
Nov. 4. 1915.	Three sick horses admitted and one discharged. Visited R.E.H. & A.S.C. lines and requisitioned details horses to be sent into section for examination.	J.S.
Nov. 5. 1915.	A.D.V.S. visited Section. Eighteen sick horses evacuated to R.E. Hospital and seven sick horses admitted. Returns rendered. One mule horse and R.E. E.H.	J.S.
Nov. 6. 1915.	Two sick horses admitted, one destroyed, and three sent towards Returns rendered. Two received asking for Return of horses. A.D.V.S. visited and arrived for mule disposed. We A.C.E.H. horse visited.	J.S.

(9 29 6) W 4141—463 100,000 9/14 H W V Forms/C. 2118/10

Army Form C. 2118.

WAR DIARY
or
INTELLIGENCE SUMMARY.
(Erase heading not required.)

Instructions regarding War Diaries and Intelligence Summaries are contained in F.S. Regs., Part II. and the Staff Manual respectively. Title pages will be prepared in manuscript.

Hour, Date, Place	Summary of Events and Information	Remarks and references to Appendices
Nov. 7th 1915 NOEUX LES MINES	Sour bran admitted. A.D.V.S. visited section. R.S.F. lines visited, also R.E.H.	J.S.
Nov. 8th 1915	Lieut. Raymond returned from leave. A.D.V.S. visited section and took description of the horses found by 1/3 R.E. and sent into section. Seven cases admitted, two one destroyed. A.S.C. lines visited. Causes for evacuation determined.	J.S.
Nov. 9th 1915	A.V.S. visited section. Twenty three horses evacuated, nineteen admitted sick, one Horse returned to duty. A.D.V.S. lines visited. 3 July three horses from 13th 18th 14th Bty. 6 R.F.A. taken to station and destroyed, three horses sick admitted.	J.S.
Nov. 10th 1915		J.S.
Nov. 11th 1915.	D.D.V.S. & A.D.V.S. visited section in morning. Seven sick horses admitted. Our pumping positions inspected with view to obtaining some for mobile Vet. Sections.	J.S.
Nov. 12th 1915	Very wet day Fifteen horses admitted sick, and one destroyed. Shot as it refused to feed and could not be found.	J.S.

Army Form C. 2118.

WAR DIARY
or
INTELLIGENCE SUMMARY.
(Erase heading not required.)

Instructions regarding War Diaries and Intelligence Summaries are contained in F.S. Regs., Part II. and the Staff Manual respectively. Title pages will be prepared in manuscript.

Hour, Date, Place	Summary of Events and Information	Remarks and references to Appendices
Nov. 13th 1915 NŒUX LES MINES	A.D.V.S. & Lieut. Gray visited Section. Thirty one horses evacuated this area a.m. etc. A.S.C. & S.H. lines visited. Returns rendered.	J.S.
Nov 14th 1915	I.D.V.S. with newly appointed D.D.V.S. and A.D.V.S. visited Section. Wagon from A.S.C. procured by A.D.V.S. and a team of equipment taken by Sergt. Ramment, who had been detailed to find a spike in new Divisional Area. Thursday. Returns rendered.	J.S.
Nov. 15th 1915 MENSECQ.	Section here from NŒUX LES MINES to site temporarily allotted at MENSECQ. Nothing of importance happened, journey actual was accomplished in a satisfactory manner. Casualties were retained for 3 horses and one mule left behind in charge of No.2. M.V.S. Provisions. These animals were unfit to make the journey.	J.S.
Nov 16th /15 " "	A.A.Q.M.G. with A.P.M. visited section. Lines prepared for horses. Carriages erected for forage, stores equipment. A.S.C. visited. Also A.D.V.S. at Hillières.	J.S.
Nov. 17th 1915 " "	A.D.V.S. visited Section. Acco. and new raid. Horse belonging 4th Devon. kept and unfit to march to station. Men sent to assess animals.	J.S.

Army Form C. 2118.

WAR DIARY
or
INTELLIGENCE SUMMARY.
(Erase heading not required.)

Instructions regarding War Diaries and Intelligence Summaries are contained in F.S. Regs., Part II. and the Staff Manual respectively. Title pages will be prepared in manuscript.

Hour, Date, Place	Summary of Events and Information	Remarks and references to Appendices
Nov. 18th 1915. MENSECQ.	Visited Divisional Train and K.E.H. lines	J.S.
Nov. 19th 1915. "	Admitted 1. Half section moved out to at Rombert. Visited ADVS. Received orders to render veterinary assistance to 3a and 4 Coy of Lond. Furniture.	J.S.
	Return rendered. Visited ADVS. Received orders to collect 3 horses. Also left to 140th Bde Brigade also to collect 3 horses. Also left at BUSNES by 93rd Divisional Train. The left at GUARBECQUE (Received) were from ADVS to proceed by LAHORE Divisional remounts accompanying by train to LILLERS to meet DAQMG. AFA 2000 rendered. Went to LILLERS pass	
Nov. 20th 1915 "	Went to BUSNES in morning collected one horses after state over to GUARBECQUE saw a horse left by the LAHORE Divisional Train. Rode back to LILLERS received afloat and proceeded) to BUSNES in afternoon and collected the second horse (Received orders from ADVS to replace Returns replace from NOEUX LES MINES collect a horse.	J.S.
Nov. 21st 1915 "	A.D.V.S. pared section and orders a horse left by Lahore Div: Train at Ham-en-Artois who collected in a float. Fortiers sick horses admitted	J.S.

Army Form C. 2118.

WAR DIARY
or
INTELLIGENCE SUMMARY.
(Erase heading not required.)

Instructions regarding War Diaries and Intelligence Summaries are contained in F.S. Regs., Part II. and the Staff Manual respectively. Title pages will be prepared in manuscript.

Hour, Date, Place	Summary of Events and Information	Remarks and references to Appendices
Nov 22nd 1915. MENSECQ	Sixty nine horses evacuated to ABBEVILLE, including forty-six Cast by D.D.R.	[signature]
Nov 23rd 1915. "	Thirty eight horses admitted. One destroyed with epizootic lymph. Visited Hd.Qtrs. 4 Battalion.	[signature]
	Transof.officer of 1 Battalion visited Leaton and wanted to see a horse from A.P.M. One cast admitted and one destroyed with lymph. Visited Hd.Qtrs. R.E.H & G.R. Batt. & 4th Batt.	[signature]
Nov 24th 1915. "	Sixteen sick horses evacuated. Seventeen sick horses admitted. T.O. 9 Batt. with Senior Chaplain visited peoling at A.P.M. hours. Six for broken horse lines chew and cuprew preprared. Visited Hd.Qtrs. 7th & 15th Battalions	[signature]
Nov 25th 1915. "	Eighteen horses admitted, including two cases of suspected mange. Seventeen examined under microscope and sent in to the Corps. mange. T.O. 17 Batt. called in consultn. certification of two mules. Visited Hd.q.Btrs. R.E.M. 4th & 15th Battns.	[signature]
Nov 26th 1915. "	Train Purrio visited. Sixteen are relieved. Clipping machine from Tyoul Sort. Twenty sick horses evacuated, including three cast by D.D.R. One horse died - pneumonia. Returns rendered. Visited Hd.Qtrs. 7 Battalion	[signature]

Army Form C. 2118.

WAR DIARY
or
INTELLIGENCE SUMMARY.
(Erase heading not required.)

Instructions regarding War Diaries and Intelligence Summaries are contained in F. S. Regs., Part II. and the Staff Manual respectively. Title pages will be prepared in manuscript.

Hour, Date, Place	Summary of Events and Information	Remarks and references to Appendices
Nov. 27th 1915 MENSECR.	Returns rendered. Adj. & met D.A.Q.M.G. at Killers and inspect remounts. Col. Jopp's Clerys sent Indelia to be clipped — punctioned. Post orderly & Telegram/Steno for pairing limits received, limits notified.	J.S.
Nov. 28th 1915 "	Op. machine returned to Col. Jopp. Gen. met news remitted. 6th & 15th Batt. news quilted also K.F.A. Returns rendered. N.C.O. men paid.	J.S.
Nov. 29th 1915 "	A.S. wagon supplies from Sis. Train Arrangements made for "Track" to take place on the morrow. Stifles news remitted, and 19 evacuated. Visited Headquarters.	J.S.
Nov. 30th 1915 "	Owing to bad weather track postponed for 24 hrs. E.S. wagon returned to Sis. Train. Visited Headquarters also 4 Batt. lines.	J.S.

101/7999

CONFIDENTIAL

WAR DIARY

of

N°2 MOBILE VETERINARY SECTION

47 London IIY

From 1-12-15 to 31-12-15

Vol IV

Army Form C. 2118.

Of Mobile Veterinary Section
47 London Division

WAR DIARY
or
INTELLIGENCE SUMMARY.
(Erase heading not required.)

Hour, Date, Place	Summary of Events and Information	Remarks and references to Appendices
December 1st 1915 MENSECQ.	Section moved on trek, leaving in charge one N.C.O. with 24 men. Ordered for timber to horse standings sent to C.R.E.	J.S.
Dec. 2nd 1915 "	2 men returned, minus one N.C.O. who was left behind in charge of cargo belonging to A.A. + Q.M.G. at Mortier. One man sent to take place of man for A.D.V.S.	J.S.
Dec. 3rd 1915 "	Two trek spinters fetched for horse standings. Returns rendered. Visited headquarters, and Mortier. Seven cases admitted. Returns rendered. Noted R.E.H.	J.S.
Dec. 4th 1915 "	Visited 6th + 5th Batt. lines also horse standings. Returns rendered. Two cases admitted.	J.S.
Dec. 5th 1915 "	Seven cases admitted. Trucks unavailable as billets for evacuation, owing to movement of troops. Seven cases admitted. Returns rendered. N.C.O. + two men traced 6 + 9 Batt. lines. A.D.V.S. paid section in afternoon. Made a Mortier arrangements made for return of A.A. + Q.M.G. charge. Twenty one horses evacuated to Lillers. Guild description.	J.S.
Dec. 6th 1915 "	9 horses evacuated sent with them. See extra starting issued to each N.C.O. + man. A.D.V.S. visited section and inspected horses for evacuation.	J.S.

Army Form C. 2118.

WAR DIARY
or
INTELLIGENCE SUMMARY.
(Erase heading not required.)

Instructions regarding War Diaries and Intelligence Summaries are contained in F. S. Regs., Part II. and the Staff Manual respectively. Title pages will be prepared in manuscript.

Hour, Date, Place	Summary of Events and Information	Remarks and references to Appendices
December 7th 1915. Tincuy.	Visited MARTHES. Slop receipt note for the horses collected. Brush bindery continued. (Clipping of machine horses.) Labour routine.	[initials]
December 9th 1915 "	ADVS visited. Eastern remounts (remena) at LILLERS. Eighteen sick horses evacuated to No 1st Vet Hospital Allerville.	[initials]
December 9th 1915 "	Brick staining continued. Application for timber for covering horse standings sent to C.R.E. Visited lines of 9th & 10th Battalions.	[initials]
December 10th 1915 "	Return received. Twenty horses evacuated to Allerville. Visited 4th Cav Bde. Three men went on leave.	[initials]
December 11th 1915 "	Return received. The barn in which men slept was flooded during the previous night. They had to wear respirators and a Cpl in Orderly Room. Blankets relatively patinated. A.D.V.S. 15 D.H. visited section. Horses put on brisk standings.	[initials]
December 12th 1915 "	Return received. Twenty six horses evacuated to Allerville. Visited 4 Cav. Bde. 9th 13th lines.	[initials]

Army Form C. 2118.

WAR DIARY
or
INTELLIGENCE SUMMARY.
(Erase heading not required.)

Instructions regarding War Diaries and Intelligence Summaries are contained in F.S. Regs., Part II. and the Staff Manual respectively. Title pages will be prepared in manuscript.

Hour, Date, Place	Summary of Events and Information	Remarks and references to Appendices
December 13th 1915 MENSECQ.	Seven horses clipped throats and evacuated for mange. 1st Sgt. Rr. Lim visited.	J.S.
December 14th 1915 "	Twenty two horses evacuated Treckville. Wagons packed ready for moving in the morning. N.E. H. Lims visited.	J.S.
December 15th 1915 IROUVIN	Section moved to Irouvin to relieve section by 15 Div. M.V.S. Fountains and horses unfit to travel, taken out. A.D.V.S. visited section in evening.	J.S.
December 16th 1915 "	A.D.V.S. visited section, Horses left by 15th examined. Major Hudson visited section as billets for another Section that was moving into same area.	J.S.
December 17th 1915 "	Visited No1. Cop. A.S.C. to see horse kicked during night. Horse had a broken leg and was destroyed. Returns rendered. Sixteen horses evacuated Treckville, two men forwarded on leave. Section horses better until trailers – no reaction.	J.S.
December 18th 1915 "	Returns rendered. Visited A.D.V.S. Lieut. Baylow going. Visited horses left behind at Allouage – unfit to travel.	J.S.
December 19th 1915 "	Returns rendered. Sixty eight horses evacuated. Forty eight horses sent to station where particulars were taken. These men returned from leave, having been attached at Boulogne for five days.	J.S.

Army Form C. 2118.

WAR DIARY
or
INTELLIGENCE SUMMARY.
(Erase heading not required.)

Instructions regarding War Diaries and Intelligence Summaries are contained in F. S. Regs., Part II. and the Staff Manual respectively. Title pages will be prepared in manuscript.

Hour, Date, Place	Summary of Events and Information	Remarks and references to Appendices
December 20th 1915 Serain	Sick men were admitted, and one died - pneumonia. Visited A.S.C. and R.E.M. keeping tabs of suspected mange.	J.J.
December 21st 1915	Nine sick men were evacuated. A.B.V.S. visited posture, felt alarm for new stock for infectious cases. Horses of Signal Co Mallines.	J.J.
December 22nd 1915 "	Sig. Co horses inspected. Three sick cases admitted K.E.H. horses Mallines.	J.J.
December 23rd 1915 "	Horses belonging to the Life Staff Mallines. Eight sick cases admitted. Infectious A.S.C. lines inspected. Returns rendered.	J.J.
December 24th 1915 "	Charges of K.E.H. Headquarters & Sig. Co. Mallines. Two sick cases admitted. Returns rendered.	J.J.
December 25th 1915 "	A.B.V.S. addressed N.C.O.s men and farriers. Reviewing the work of M.V.S. he afterwards great satisfaction. At evening O.C. took the chair. Many toasts were proposed from orations of Vet. Officers, N.C.O.s men. Returns rendered.	J.J.

(9 29 6) W 4141—463 100,000 9/14 H W V Forms/C. 2118/10

Army Form C. 2118.

WAR DIARY
or
INTELLIGENCE SUMMARY.
(Erase heading not required.)

Instructions regarding War Diaries and Intelligence Summaries are contained in F. S. Regs., Part II. and the Staff Manual respectively. Title pages will be prepared in manuscript.

Hour, Date, Place	Summary of Events and Information	Remarks and references to Appendices
December 26th 1915 Rouen	Eight sick cases admitted and fourteen evacuated. Officers rounded. Visited Headquarters N.F.K.	J.S.
December 27th 1915 "	Six sick cases admitted. A.D.V.S. visited lines and inspected all horses. Visited A.S.C. N.C.O. then home.	J.S.
December 28th 1915 "	Eight cases dog admitted and few admitted. Several horses sent for new shoes.	J.S.
December 29th 1915 "	New shoes ordered by R.E. Nine sick cases admitted. Visited R.E.H.	J.S.
December 30th 1915 "	New shoes continued. A.D.V.S. visited station and inspected horses previous to evacuation. Twenty two horses evacuated. Seventeen cases admitted. Visited A.S.C.	J.S.
December 31st 1915 "	One horse died — pneumonia. Ten new horses taken on leave. Last few exceptions play was filled and easy to repair horse standings. Since coming to Rouen 2nd. Return Rendered.	J.S.

Forms/C. 2118/10

47

1/2 London Nottl. Nly Section

Jan
00 £ V

47ᵗʰ Dⁿ

Army Form C. 2118.

WAR DIARY
of
INTELLIGENCE SUMMARY.
(Erase heading not required.)

Instructions regarding War Diaries and Intelligence Summaries are contained in F.S. Regs., Part II. and the Staff Manual respectively. Title pages will be prepared in manuscript.

[Stamp: MOBILE VETERINARY SECTION No. 2 Date 31.1.16 47th LONDON DIVISION]

Hour, Date, Place	Summary of Events and Information	Remarks and references to Appendices
January 1st 1916. DROUVIN	Twenty nine horses evacuated to Abbeville, and two destroyed. Eleven sick cases admitted to section. One Sergeant officers charger received from No 1 to No 11. Visited A.S.C. A.D.V.S. visited section. One man on line picquet found unconscious apparently in fit. Return rendered.	J.S.
January 2nd 1916. "	Nine sick horses admitted, and one discharged to duty. Returns rendered. Two found ill sent to A.D.M.S. off duty for the day.	J.S.
January 3rd 1916 "	Six sick cases admitted. Visited N.F.H and A.S.C. Nil reg. no new cases.	J.S.
January 4th 1916 "	Twenty four sick cases admitted. A.D.V.S. visited section about D.V.O. and inspected a horse from Am. Clm. 6 F.A.B. that showed slight reaction to mallein but this horse was put into a pasturine loft and kept under observation, isolated.	J.S.
January 5th 1916 "	Visited A.S.C. and tested with mallein horses of No 1 Co. Thirty cases evacuated and nine admitted. Visited R.E.H	J.S.
January 6th 1916 "	A.D.V.S. visited section. Four cases admitted.	J.S.
January 7th 1916 "	Twenty eight sick cases admitted. D.A.Q.M.G. visited section to inspect horses from 47th D.A.C. as so many of the horses from this unit are admitted and recommended for debility. Mallein horses of No 2 Co. A.S.C. Twenty nine horses evacuated. Stamps rendered.	J.S.

Army Form C. 2118.

WAR DIARY
or
INTELLIGENCE SUMMARY.
(Erase heading not required.)

Instructions regarding War Diaries and Intelligence Summaries are contained in F. S. Regs., Part II. and the Staff Manual respectively. Title pages will be prepared in manuscript.

Hour, Date, Place	Summary of Events and Information	Remarks and references to Appendices
January 8th 1916. DROUVIN.	Seven sick cases admitted. A.B.T.S. visited section. Returns rendered.	A.S.
January 9th 1916. "	Six cases admitted and fifteen sick evacuated. A.B.T.S. visited section and made arrangements to carry on while O.C. was away. Return rendered. N.C.o.'s rain paid.	
January 10th 1916. "	O.C. Rest to Rest Camp. A.B.T.S. visited section and inspected all horses. Four cases admitted.	
January 11th 1916. "	A.B.T.S. visited section and inspected all horses. Nine sick admitted and one discharged. C.R.A. visited section and asked how many A.T.D.A.C. horses.	
January 12th 1916. "	A.B.T.S. visited section and ordered evacuation of twenty three cases. Nine cases admitted.	
January 13th 1916. "	A.B.T.S. visited section and examined all horses. Seven cases admitted.	
January 14th 1916. "	Returns rendered. Two men granted leave to proceed to England. A.B.T.S. visited section. Lieut. Rebrook A.V.C. taken over O.C.	

Army Form C. 2118.

WAR DIARY
or
INTELLIGENCE SUMMARY.
(Erase heading not required.)

Instructions regarding War Diaries and Intelligence Summaries are contained in F.S. Regs., Part II. and the Staff Manual respectively. Title pages will be prepared in manuscript.

Hour, Date, Place	Summary of Events and Information	Remarks and references to Appendices
January 15th 1916. DROUIN.	Returns rendered.	J.S.
January 16th 1916. DROUIN.	A.V.S. visited kestrel, and ordered the evacuation of twentynine horses. Nine cases admitted.	J.S.
	Returns Rendered. Thirteen sick cases admitted. A.V.S. visited section.	
January 14th 1916.	Eleven sick cases admitted.	J.S.
January 18th 1916.	A.V.S. visited nestors and returned the horse and prepared glanders. A client was left by him to place the temperature of this animal arrested four cars.	J.S.
	Thirty one cases sent by resound by order of A.D.V.S. Ten cases were admitted.	J.S.
January 19th 1916.	A.V.S. visited section. Six cases admitted.	J.S.
January 20th 1916.	Five cases admitted. A.V.S. visited section in afternoon. Some papers sent for G.C. and were sent on to the Base Corps.	J.S.
January 21st 1916.	Returns rendered. G.C. previous Form on leave. A.V.S. visited section. Eight sick cases admitted.	J.S.
January 22nd 1916.	A.V.S. visited section and evacuated twenty three cases. Returns rendered. Seven sick cases admitted.	C.S.

Army Form C. 2118.

WAR DIARY
or
INTELLIGENCE SUMMARY.
(Erase heading not required.)

Instructions regarding War Diaries and Intelligence Summaries are contained in F.S. Regs., Part II. and the Staff Manual respectively. Title pages will be prepared in manuscript.

Hour, Date, Place	Summary of Events and Information	Remarks and references to Appendices
January 23rd 1916 DROUVIN	Return rendered. A.V.S. practise practised, and A.D.M.S. Arrangements made for burying a horse. Three sick cases admitted.	
January 24th 1916	Eleven sick cases admitted. The horse with suspected glanders was destroyed. The A.V.S. held a post mortem on the carcase but was unable to find any symptoms of glanders or organs. The carcase was buried in lime by the S. Area Ant. Goat borrowed from M. Lebon and the horses were collected. Another horse was destroyed and returned sick frost.	
January 25th 1916 "	Six sick cases admitted. A.V.S. practised section also A.V.S. of 16 Division.	
January 26th 1916	Eleven cases admitted. A.V.S. practised Section and ordered the destruction of one horse with foundered feet.	
January 27th 1916 "	A.V.S. practised Section and ordered the evacuation of twenty four sick horse borrowed as power for two new troughs in Lour.	
January 28th 1916. "	Returns rendered. Six cases admitted. A.V.S. practised section. Capt. Whipps called here two horse admitted. One before two, and one internal.	

Army Form C. 2118.

WAR DIARY
or
INTELLIGENCE SUMMARY.
(Erase heading not required.)

Instructions regarding War Diaries and Intelligence Summaries are contained in F. S. Regs., Part II. and the Staff Manual respectively. Title pages will be prepared in manuscript.

Hour, Date, Place	Summary of Events and Information	Remarks and references to Appendices
January 29th 1916 Sporion.	Returns received. A.D.V.S. visited section and issued three pack asses to be posted before horses from 15 Division. Capt Wolffin again visited section. Sit down admitted.	J.S.
January 30th 1916 "	Returns received. A.D.V.S. visited section and left particulars of Corp men to take sick horses wagon to Albeville. Supt attend return sick a flock.	L.S.
January 31st 1916 "	Corp Phillips Pte Clifford started for Albeville with sickened wagon and three horses. A.D.V.S. visited section and issued evacuation of twenty four sick horses. Eight horses from 15 Division and horse fetched from Proeyr. & Minor.	O.S.

49

WAR DIARY

of

½ London Mobile Vet Sect'n

Vol VI

Feb 1 1916 — Feb 29 1916

CONFIDENTIAL

Army Form C. 2118.

WAR DIARY
or
INTELLIGENCE SUMMARY.
(Erase heading not required.)

MOBILE VETERINARY SECTION
No. 1/2 London
Date 1/3/16
47th LONDON DIVISION

Hour, Date, Place	Summary of Events and Information	Remarks and references to Appendices
1st February 1916 ROUEN	A.D.V.S. visited section and inspected all sick horses. No 18 L.G.R. sent 16 section from No 6. Vet. Hospital ROUEN. Why he was returned is not known. Two sick cases admitted.	J.S.
2nd February 1916 "	A.D.V.S. visited section. No horses admitted.	J.S.
3rd February 1916 "	A.D.V.S. visited section. Seven sick cases admitted. Clipping machine was returned by 4 R.W. & L. Benethens. Ordered floating in hand, canvas removed.	J.S.
4th February 1916 "	During the night the mine ramour became acute stages in the "range" also O/c. break. Three mine ruptures sick apparently. A.D.V.S. and Capt. Stuart visited section. Clipping machine lent to 4 Div Ad. Returns rendered.	J.S.
5th February 1916 "	A.D.V.S. visited section and orders evacuation of forty two sick horses. Eleven cases admitted. Returns rendered.	J.S.
6th February 1916 "	Six sick cases admitted. A.D.V.S. visited section. Returns rendered.	J.S.

Army Form C. 2118.

WAR DIARY
or
INTELLIGENCE SUMMARY.
(Erase heading not required.)

Instructions regarding War Diaries and Intelligence Summaries are contained in F. S. Regs., Part II. and the Staff Manual respectively. Title pages will be prepared in manuscript.

Hour, Date, Place	Summary of Events and Information	Remarks and references to Appendices
7th February 1916 Morning	Lieut. Shellard & Sr. Belford returned with float from Abugila. A.B.y.S. visited section and Mallams note that has been under observation. N.Con. and new pans.	
8th February 1916 "	Eight sick cases admitted. A.B.y.S. visited section and specimen mule also inspected Temperature Chart.	
9th February 1916 "	A.B.y.S. visited section in company with A.B.y.S. 16 Bd., also P.O. No. 2 M.V.S. into camp to inspect others returning before passing out. Seventeen sick cases admitted and thirty two cases evacuated. Two horses fetched in by float. A.B.y.S. visited section in afternoon, and examined mule he sent back twenty seven sick cases examined. One with p.tt. wound in hip also suffering from Tetanus.	
10th February 1916 "	A.B.y.S. visited section and viewed the horses the Jutaba by float. Six sick cases admitted. 28 horses arrived.	
12th February 1916 "	28 horses admitted. Two horses died in night. A.B.y.S. visited section and ordered evacuation of twenty two cases. Capt. Spoone + Lieut. Byrd arrived ration. Officer commanding returned from leave. Sick horses not could not be lifted with Mallams going into section and Septicaemic observation. A completed reaction isolated and Septicaemic observation.	

Forms/C. 2118/10

Army Form C. 2118.

WAR DIARY
or
INTELLIGENCE SUMMARY.
(Erase heading not required.)

Instructions regarding War Diaries and Intelligence Summaries are contained in F.S. Regs., Part II. and the Staff Manual respectively. Title pages will be prepared in manuscript.

Hour, Date, Place	Summary of Events and Information	Remarks and references to Appendices
13th February 1916 TROUIN	Returns rendered. All horses in sections examined. Mallein horses returned to their units. A.B.v.S. made instructions also Capt. Edwards; in the afternoon the A.P.M. called. The inspector general's were sent to have a typhoid inoculation.	J.S.
14th February 1916 "	Twenty-one sick horses admitted. Visits made to Co. A.S.C. and inspected horses also K.E. Horse. No one then paid.	J.S.
15th February 1916 "	Eleven sick horses admitted and forty three evacuated. Packers ready for moving to the address.	J.S.
16th February 1916 LILLERS.	The section moved from Trouin to Lillers. Twelve sick horses were handed over to No 2. M.V.S. and the men taken over from them. The day was very rough and wet.	J.S.
17th February 1916 "	Places and cleaner for horses in the new stand, as their are no cover the places no steps in the one we arm. One sick horse admitted. Eght-horses that could not be mallein in truck sent to Section to be tested. The Claims Officer made inspection.	J.S.
18th February 1916 "	Seven sick horses admitted including one fetched by boat. A.B.v.S. made inspection. Returns rendered.	J.S.

Army Form C. 2118.

WAR DIARY
or
INTELLIGENCE SUMMARY.
(Erase heading not required.)

Instructions regarding War Diaries and Intelligence Summaries are contained in F.S. Regs., Part II. and the Staff Manual respectively. Title pages will be prepared in manuscript.

Hour, Date, Place	Summary of Events and Information	Remarks and references to Appendices
19th February 1916 LILLERS	Fifteen sick horses admitted and thirteen evacuated. One horse with punctured sole taken to Abbeville destroyed. Returns rendered.	[sig]
20th February 1916 "	Four sick cases admitted. A.D.V.S. paid a visit and made instructions, three sick punctured feet to be destroyed. Returns rendered.	[sig]
21st February 1916 "	Fifteen sick cases admitted including horses left behind by the E.F.A.B. which had to be fetched by float. One horse taken habitation and destroyed. Twenty one horses evacuated.	[sig]
22nd February 1916 "	Seven sick cases admitted. Capt. Gray paid a visit.	[sig]
23rd February 1916 "	Five sick cases admitted, and several not sick enough to be admitted were moved and sent back to unit. N.C.O. & men paid. Six horses in from 11st impet Horse dis.	[sig]
24th February 1916 "	Six sick cases admitted. A.D.V.S. paid a visit. Machine for sharpening clipping machine knives supplied.	[sig]

Army Form C. 2118.

WAR DIARY
or
INTELLIGENCE SUMMARY.
(Erase heading not required.)

Instructions regarding War Diaries and Intelligence Summaries are contained in F. S. Regs., Part II. and the Staff Manual respectively. Title pages will be prepared in manuscript.

Hour, Date, Place	Summary of Events and Information	Remarks and references to Appendices
25th February 1916 LILLERS.	J.D.V.S. with A.V.S. visited stables and inspected sheep and horses. Two Remounts — one a mule and a heavy contused knee — turned over to station. One sick horse admitted. Returns rendered.	J.S.
26th February 1916 LILLERS.	9 Listers pick horses as admitted. Sick mare admitted including one fetched by float. One horse died — senecitis. One horse with fracture of hip destroyed and one at Lozinghem. Returns rendered.	J.S.
27th February 1916 "	One sick horse admitted, and one died. Returns rendered. A.V.S. visited station.	J.S.
28th February 1916 "	One mule received from BUSNES that has been left by an unknown Unit since November 1915. Receipt sent to left. Six sick horses admitted.	J.S.
29th February 1916 "	Twelve sick horses admitted including one fetched by float. Lpl. Muckitt returned from leave. Returns rendered. A.V.S. visited station.	J.S.

47

WAR DIARY
of
½ London Mobile Vet. Section

Vol VII

From 1.3.16 to 31. 3. 16.

CONFIDENTIAL

Army Form C. 2118.

WAR DIARY
or
INTELLIGENCE SUMMARY.
(Erase heading not required.)

Instructions regarding War Diaries and Intelligence Summaries are contained in F.S. Regs., Part II. and the Staff Manual respectively. Title pages will be prepared in manuscript.

MOBILE VETERINARY SECTION
No. 2 London
Date 1. 3. 1916.
47th LONDON DIVN

Hour, Date, Place	Summary of Events and Information	Remarks and references to Appendices
1st March 1916. LILLERS.	Twenty one horses Evacuated. One was impossible to dispose of the carcase pthomais, they had to be buried. A post mortem should reveal due to enteritis. N.C.o. and men fair.	J.S.
2nd March 1916. "	O.C. 47 M.V.S. called to ask permission to proceed the float convoy to the Section. Visited Abbatoir. Section Horse kicked during night. Scratch seen to Abbatoir and destroyed - fractured tibia. Horse will dispose slaughter to Abbatoir and destroyed.	J.S.
3rd March 1916. "	Visited R.F.H. Capt Craig v Ryan painted Section. Panelled horse floated in by No. 47 M.V.S. N.C.o. men sent to Battn. Returns rendered.	J.S.
4th March 1916. "	Thirteen sick horses evacuated. Rain and snow, horses are now of shed in which sick horses were standing. Visited R.E.H. Returns rendered.	J.S.
5th March 1916. "	Sergeant in charge of the men with float to collect the horses left behind at Enq. St Julien. Both sick horses were able to walk. Several horses of ashes fetched for shed that was flooded. Returns rendered.	J.S.

WAR DIARY
or
INTELLIGENCE SUMMARY.
(Erase heading not required.)

Army Form C. 2118.

Instructions regarding War Diaries and Intelligence Summaries are contained in F. S. Regs., Part II. and the Staff Manual respectively. Title pages will be prepared in manuscript.

Hour, Date, Place	Summary of Events and Information	Remarks and references to Appendices
6th March 1916. LILLERS.	The two horses floated in by No.47 M.V.S. on 2nd inst. Taken to Abbatoir and destroyed with permission from A.D.V.S. 16 Div. The horses being free from lice, horses taken for long exercise ride.	J.J.
7th March 1916. "	A.D.V.S. 16 Div. visited section to see what accommodation there was, as his M.V.S. were taking over.	J.J.
8th March 1916. "	Twenty two horses evacuated. A.D.V.S. 16 Div. and O.C. No.47 M.V.S. again visited section and inspected stables and billets. O.C. confirms to take such horses into A.D.V.S. visited BRUAY to find site for section.	J.J.
9th March 1916. BRUAY.	Section moved to BRUAY and occupied stables vacated by French troops. There stores were disinfected with flowlong and spray supplies by R.S.P.C.A. Billets found for N.C.Os. men. O.C. turned to clearing house for fourteen seat.	J.J.
10th March 1916. "	Stores again disinfected and lime washed. Sgt. sent to Auchel to fetch horse. Returns rendered.	J.J.
11th March 1916. "	A.D.V.S. visited section and found stables for infectious cases. This was disinfected with flowlong, spray and lime washed. Cpl. from 23 C/H. called to collect horse and report progress of another belonging to H.Q. 23 C/H. Returns rendered.	J.J.

Army Form C. 2118.

WAR DIARY
or
INTELLIGENCE SUMMARY.
(Erase heading not required.)

Instructions regarding War Diaries and Intelligence Summaries are contained in F. S. Regs., Part II. and the Staff Manual respectively. Title pages will be prepared in manuscript.

Hour, Date, Place	Summary of Events and Information	Remarks and references to Appendices
12th March 1916 BRUAY.	A.D.V.S. visited practice. Returns rendered. Veterinary Memo for units #7 Div. arrived. Orders sent notifying the various O.C.'s concerned.	J.S.
13th March 1916 "	A.D.V.S. visited Practice and sent note A.T.S. N.C.O. man pain.	J.S.
14th March 1916 "	N.C.O. man sent to collect two horses at Cojeque and remain the night. Cart sent to KILLERS to collect O.C's baggage. Arrangements made for evacuation but horses arrived too late. N.C.O. man from No 3rd M.V.S. 23 Div arrived to take over chas. chelets.	J.S.
15th March 1916 "	N.C. returned to station. A.D.V.S. 2 Div. with O.C. M.V.S. also O.C. 3rd M.V.S. practice stations to make arrangements for taking over. N.C.O. sent back with officer to take over two sick horses from two sick horses evacuated.	J.S.
16th March 1916 Caucourt	Station in company with A.D.V.S. moved to CAUCOURT. The horses taken over were extremely dirty. Hugs heaps of manure along each side of sheds. Men proposed up to keep it from falling.	J.S.

(9 29 6) W 4141—463 100,000 9/14 HWV Forms/C. 2118/10

Army Form C. 2118.

WAR DIARY
or
INTELLIGENCE SUMMARY.
(Erase heading not required.)

Instructions regarding War Diaries and Intelligence Summaries are contained in F.S. Regs., Part II. and the Staff Manual respectively. Title pages will be prepared in manuscript.

Hour, Date, Place	Summary of Events and Information	Remarks and references to Appendices
17th March 1916 Carencourt	Cart sent to Hersin station for Laundry Party. Two horses from 23 Div taken in as that unit was under orders to move. Capt. Edwards invalid station. Return rendered.	J.S.
18th March 1916 "	Burying Certificate sent for Bruay-killers. Two sick cases admitted. Return rendered.	J.S.
19th March 1916 "	Sent out to fetch horses from 8 Corps also three others – horses horses. The unit to which these horses belonged could not be found. In afternoon sent out again to collect another horse from 23 Div. Twelve sick cases admitted. Return rendered.	J.S.
20th March 1916 "	NCO sent to Bruay to No. 35 M.V.S. to collect horses left partially rationed by this division. Fifteen sick cases admitted, including eight treated from Gurkha kyel belonging to 23 Div.	J.S.
21st March 1916 "	Orders received to move on the morrow. Four sick cases admitted.	J.S.
22nd March 1916 HERIPRE	Skelyo moved to Heripré. Demand cases unable to walk affts. lorries. Stopping for horse wire investigating Sick horses had the kick in the open. Shot sent to collect horses from 17 R.G.A. Regs. rendered.	J.S.
23rd March 1916 "	Horses left at Carencourt pickets loaded. Visited R.E.H. and manure horses for evacuation to arrive by 9 am.	J.S.

Forms/C. 2118/10

Army Form C. 2118.

WAR DIARY
or
INTELLIGENCE SUMMARY.
(Erase heading not required.)

Instructions regarding War Diaries and Intelligence Summaries are contained in F.S. Regs., Part II. and the Staff Manual respectively. Title pages will be prepared in manuscript.

Hour, Date, Place	Summary of Events and Information	Remarks and references to Appendices
24 March 1916 HERIDRE.	Graunted. 3.9 pack horses. Snow fell in night so made it necessary to find shelter for sick horses. 7 cases of mortal from same received. These were many only. Horses collected from Cambrai Chateau. Returns rendered. Horses that did not arrive in time for evacuation, returned to units.	J.L.
25 March 1916 "	Snow fell again during the night and continued throughout the day. Returns rendered. Three sick cases admitted.	J.L.
26th March 1916 "	Snow fell during night and continued during the day at intervals. Two sick cases admitted. Returns rendered.	J.L.
27th March 1916 "	Rain and sleet fell during day causing snow to disappear. Visited L.E.H.	J.L.
28th March 1916 FRESNICOURT	A.D.V.S. visited section at midday and moved normal of section to Grenicourt. Section moved at 3 p.m. N.C.O. man left in charge of Grenicourt horses. Shoes and surroundings very dirty. Seven sick cases admitted.	J.L.
29th March 1916 "	Clean sick cases admitted. A.D.V.S. called. Two horses left at Hersin. No medical to section.	J.L.
30th March 1916 "	A.D.V.S. with A.D.V.S. called in afternoon. Sorty two horses inspected. Eighteen sick cases admitted. Two horses sent to Bethune and slaughtered.	J.L.
31st March 1916 "	A.D.V.S. visited section. Three horses and mules from September. Q.S. wagon and horses supplies for A.O.D. to Lillers and manure. Returns rendered.	J.L.

WAR DIARY

of

½ London Mobile Vet. Section
47th London Div.

Vol VIII

From 1-4-16 to 30-4-16

Confidential

Army Form C. 2118.

WAR DIARY
INTELLIGENCE SUMMARY.
(Erase heading not required.)

Instructions regarding War Diaries and Intelligence Summaries are contained in F.S. Regs., Part II. and the Staff Manual respectively. Title pages will be prepared in manuscript.

MOBILE VETERINARY SECTION
No. ....
Date 1.4.16
47th LONDON DIVISION

Place	Date	Hour	Summary of Events and Information	Remarks and references to Appendices
FRESNICOURT	April 1		Sick horse admitted. No 35 Pvt. Kedden admitted sick returned in hospital.	
"	2		A.D.S. visits patient. Return received. Removal of manure continued. Pvt. Kedden evacuated. Visited Hd. Qrs. & Corps Returns received. Services cases admitted.	
"	3		Four men recommended for promotion to sergeants to be attached to T.F.A. Brigades in accordance with instructions received. Visited K.E.H. and inspected horses, stopped pases into division to have their teeth attended to.	
"	4		Sick horse admitted. K.E.H. horse examined and teeth filed. Visited 2 Res. Park A.S.C. Again mine fired.	
"	5		Sin sick cases admitted. Return of Pvt. Kedden sent to A.S.C. Burras Secn. Removal of manure continued. Visited and inspected horses of D.A.C. No 18 Lcpl. Ralf, reinforcement from Havre.	
"	6		Pit sick cases admitted. A.D.V.S. called prior to his going on leave early the following morning. Visited H.Q. & Corps and K.E.H.	
"	7		Sixteen sick cases admitted and forty horses and two mules evacuated. Station was being shelled while horses were being loaded. Visited Divisional Train.	

T2134. Wt. W708—778. 500000. 4/15. Sir J. C. & S.

WAR DIARY
INTELLIGENCE SUMMARY.
(Erase heading not required.)

Army Form C. 2118.

Instructions regarding War Diaries and Intelligence Summaries are contained in F. S. Regs., Part II. and the Staff Manual respectively. Title pages will be prepared in manuscript.

Place	Date	Hour	Summary of Events and Information	Remarks and references to Appendices
FRESNICOURT	April 8		Visited office of A.D.V.S. to sign papers. Returns rendered. Buried dung, called over and converted into a flower bed. One sick horse admitted. Returns rendered.	
	9		Returns rendered. Visited H.Q. 1st Corps in response to wire. & wire met very solid frosts interfered with work of clearing up the camp.	
	10		Say the sick horse taken on the range and put through a course of musketry. Six sick horses admitted.	
	11		Remained at station. Taken to range and instructed in musketry. A very trying afternoon. Four sick horses admitted. Visited A.D.V.S. office.	
	12		Clean park horse admitted including now cases sent by D.D.V. Knowles horses and two mules evacuated. Lieut Payne met at Station and conducted to this section. Lieut Smyth called for instructions and papers to proceed home to England his relief being offered. Visited L.E.H and H.Q. 1st Corps.	

Army Form C. 2118.

WAR DIARY
INTELLIGENCE SUMMARY
(Erase heading not required.)

Instructions regarding War Diaries and Intelligence Summaries are contained in F. S. Regs., Part II. and the Staff Manual respectively. Title pages will be prepared in manuscript.

Place	Date	Hour	Summary of Events and Information	Remarks and references to Appendices
FRESNICOURT	April 13		Veterinary Officers for various units arrived for distribution. Units so nominated were notified by wire. Went out to Divisional Train to collect horse with open tack.	J.G.
"	14		Sore neck case admitted including one fitted by foot suffering from a punctured foot. Leave stopped. Sergt Moreth reported for England. Having to report at St Albans Hospital. New men from Returns received. 3 Co. Pet visited.	J.G.
"	15		Horse collected by float on previous day taken to Division and distributed. No 3 Vet LMH much admitted to hospital with septic hand. Sent for Veterinary Officer.	J.G.
"	16		Forwarded for approval returns received. Returns received. Visited R.F.H. & A.V. Colln. & Corps	J.G.
"	17		S.D. Waggon returned from Divisional Train and a supply of spares obtained to repair standings in sheds. Divn sick cases admitted. Visited Divisional Train & Co. Ps.	J.G.
"	18		Attended horse on loan to p. 2 Dr Pearson that was kicked during night. Horse was destroyed suffering from fractured radius. Fifteen sick horses admitted.	J.G.

T2131. Wt. W708—776. 500000. 4/15. Sir J. C. & S.

Army Form C. 2118.

WAR DIARY
or
INTELLIGENCE SUMMARY.
(Erase heading not required.)

Instructions regarding War Diaries and Intelligence Summaries are contained in F. S. Regs., Part II. and the Staff Manual respectively. Title pages will be prepared in manuscript.

Place	Date	Hour	Summary of Events and Information	Remarks and references to Appendices
FRESNICOURT	April 19		Sick cases admitted and twenty three horses and two mules evacuated. Eight few remounts examined at station. A.P.V.S. visited [station] and left [packet] of flowerpots.	
"	20		Sick cases admitted. A.P.V.S. visited section. Visited S. & M.	
"	21		Lf/Lt Mackett discharged from hospital. Took cart to collect horse with punctured foot. Field ambulance placed of manure after many days work. Returns rendered.	
"	22		A.P.V.S. visited section. Horses selected by Staph on 13 mod. destroyed otherwise. Returns rendered.	
"	23		Sick cases admitted. Returns rendered. Sic sick cases admitted. Visited H.Q. a Corps.	
"	24		Sick cases admitted. Visited Divisional Train also 2 Sec Park.	
"	25		A.M.S. has made representation from which horses are evacuated to small reserved started to keep a supply of water in case steam fails. Sick men with teeth trouble to meet the Hd Dent Cart. S.C.16 to receive attention. Ten sick cases admitted.	

Army Form C. 2118.

WAR DIARY
INTELLIGENCE SUMMARY.
(Erase heading not required.)

Instructions regarding War Diaries and Intelligence Summaries are contained in F. S. Regs., Part II. and the Staff Manual respectively. Title pages will be prepared in manuscript.

Place	Date	Hour	Summary of Events and Information	Remarks and references to Appendices
FRESNICOURT	26		Seven sick cases admitted and twenty two horses and three mules evacuated. One mare foaled on way to Abbeville. reply.	J.S.
"	27		Pte Rollo severe Duty suffering with piles. Water supply continued. Message received from H.R. H Capt to examine dog for suspected Rabies. One sick case admitted. Doinyh Lewis & Pte J Brother proceeded on leave. Another hay now never steam to keep a good supply of water. Visited K.E.H. and 27. F.A. Returns rendered.	J.S.
"	28			J.S.
"	29		A.D.V.S. visited section also Capts Bryan & Clarke for further advice on horse suffering with an abscess on breast. Four sick cases admitted. Returns rendered.	J.S.
"	30		Returns rendered. Visited 1 C.A.C.C. to see horse dangerously ill with tetanus. Horse slightly better in morning. One sick case admitted. All N.Cos and men medically examined for perhic. Eight full pay books A.B.64 forwarded to Paymaster.	J.S.

WAR DIARY

MOBILE VETERINARY SECTION
47th London DIV.

From 1.5.16
To 31.5.16

Army Form C. 2118.

WAR DIARY
of
INTELLIGENCE SUMMARY.
(Erase heading not required.)

Instructions regarding War Diaries and Intelligence Summaries are contained in F. S. Regs., Part II. and the Staff Manual respectively. Title pages will be prepared in manuscript.

Place	Date	Hour	Summary of Events and Information	Remarks and references to Appendices
FRESNICOURT	MAY 1		D.D.V.S. with A.D.V.S. visited the section and inspected horse ambulance. Visited A.D.C. in morning and again in evening taking a post mortem on horse that died suddenly; cause of death liver of small intestine. Three rugs and 3rd blanket returned to Railhead. Two sick cases admitted	J.S.
"	2		Visited A.D.C. also 'R' Bty at Troce 9 in response to urgent telephone message at midnight. Orders received to collect all 54 Ell Vet. Chests from units. Four sick cases admitted.	J.S.
"	3		Visited "R" Bty. to see urgent case, also 2 Rn Park, also + Corps H.Q. also K.F.H. A.D.V.S. visited Section in evening took photos received. Two sick cases admitted	J.S.
"	4		Visited A.D.C. also + Corps H.Q. also 'R' Bty at Berles Visited A.D.C. again an urgent case. A.D.V.S. visited Section Three sick cases admitted	J.S.

Army Form C. 2118.

WAR DIARY
or
INTELLIGENCE SUMMARY.
(Erase heading not required.)

Instructions regarding War Diaries and Intelligence Summaries are contained in F. S. Regs., Part II. and the Staff Manual respectively. Title pages will be prepared in manuscript.

Place	Date	Hour	Summary of Events and Information	Remarks and references to Appendices
FRESNICOURT	MAY 5		Returns received. Horse sent to lines of 15 Bde. to collect lame horse. Two sick cases admitted.	J.G.
	6		Returns received. Horse sent to lines of 16 Bde. to collect lame horse. A.D.V.S. visited station and inspected controls of Vet. Sheds received in orders to send in his report. Thirty sick horses evacuated from train. Thirteen cases admitted, including one horse found by H.Q.	L.G.
	7		Returns received. Horse sent to collect sick horse from E Sorrow. One sick case admitted. One horse returned from leave.	W.
	8		Visited 4 Corps H.Q., also K.E.H., also 2 Rio O.H., also K.E.H. Vet sheds sent to bring horse from strain. A.D.V.S. visited section. South horses returned from leave. Nine sick cases admitted.	J.G.
	9		Visited A.D.V.S. r K.E.H. Horse sent to collect lame horse from 13 Bde. Two sick horses admitted.	J.G.

T2131. Wt. W708—776. 500000. 4/15. Siv. J. C. & S.

Army Form C. 2118.

WAR DIARY
or
INTELLIGENCE SUMMARY.
(Erase heading not required.)

Instructions regarding War Diaries and Intelligence Summaries are contained in F. S. Regs., Part II. and the Staff Manual respectively. Title pages will be prepared in manuscript.

Place	Date	Hour	Summary of Events and Information	Remarks and references to Appendices
FRESNICOURT	MAY. 10		Field service kits collected and returned to Ordnance	J.S.
"	11		Visited A.D.C. and #Coyps. H.Q. Visited Field Cashier. Four sick cases admitted.	J.S.
"	12		Visited A.D.C. Left Coy proceed on leave. Seven sick cases admitted.	J.S.
"	13		Twenty new sick horses evacuated. Visited A.D.B. in afternoon and again in evening, also 260 R. Returns rendered. Eight sick cases admitted.	J.S.
"	14		Returns rendered. Visited A.D.C. and #Coyps H.Q. One sick case admitted and one taken to Arras and disposed. 120 ft received for extension.	J.S.
"	15		Returns rendered. Visited A.D.C. in morning and again in afternoon. Two sick cases admitted.	J.S.

Army Form C. 2118.

WAR DIARY
INTELLIGENCE SUMMARY.
(Erase heading not required.)

Instructions regarding War Diaries and Intelligence Summaries are contained in F. S. Regs., Part II. and the Staff Manual respectively. Title pages will be prepared in manuscript.

Place	Date	Hour	Summary of Events and Information	Remarks and references to Appendices
	MAY.			
FRESNICOURT	15		Visited A.S.C. in morning also 2 Res Pk. Visited A.D.S. again in evening and found three had died. Seven sick cases admitted.	
"	16		Visited A.D.S. and held P.M. on horse. Important F. A.D.S. Fastest horse with punctured foot. Vet. other advice from R.A.V. units notified. Harness repairs and collection from A.C.S. A.V.S. visited Section in evening. Three sick cases admitted. Sick Horse at 2 Res Pk reported.	
"	17		Visited H Corps HQ also 2 Res Pk. and held P.M. on horse that died sudden in the previous night. Visited Brits Cashel and said N.C.O.'s men. Six sick cases admitted.	
"	18		Visited A.D.S. Two sick cases admitted.	
"	19.		Skirting A.V.C. drafts arrived at Section from England, and await instructions. Visited 2 Res Pk and A.S.C., who visited Section in evening, and lectured the visitors re duties. Have been taking both rows and Australia – 12 oft. P[unclear] cases admitted. No 31. Gnr. L. Twacktaranater.	

Army Form C. 2118.

WAR DIARY
INTELLIGENCE SUMMARY.
(Erase heading not required.)

Instructions regarding War Diaries and Intelligence Summaries are contained in F. S. Regs., Part II. and the Staff Manual respectively. Title pages will be prepared in manuscript.

Place	Date	Hour	Summary of Events and Information	Remarks and references to Appendices
FRESNICOURT	MAY 20		Returns rendered. Visited Corps H.Q. dental dept. posted to Hers unite. One sick case admitted. One mule - a suspicious case - tested with mallein - no result.	J.S.
"	21		Returns rendered. Four sick cases admitted.	J.S.
"	22		Host sent to 22 C.D.L. lines to collect horse suffering from abort wounds. Three more sheep horses cases admitted and twenty perm. cases evacuated from therein. Visited V.Q.L.	J.S.
"	23		Host sent to A236 Bty. to collect horse with glub was. One cow destroyed at Herouin - 12 of H. and nine sick cases admitted. Visited Corps H.Q. also 2 Res Pk.	J.S.
"	24		O.R.S. visited section. Eight sick cases admitted.	J.S.
"	25		Host sent to 237 B.A.C. to collect horse with centered knee. Ten sick cases admitted. Visited D.D.S. also 2 Res Pk.	J.S.

T.J.134. Wt. W708-776. 500000. 4/15. Sir J. C. & S.

Army Form C. 2118.

WAR DIARY
INTELLIGENCE SUMMARY.
(Erase heading not required.)

Instructions regarding War Diaries and Intelligence Summaries are contained in F.S. Regs., Part II. and the Staff Manual respectively. Title pages will be prepared in manuscript.

Place	Date	Hour	Summary of Events and Information	Remarks and references to Appendices
FRESNICOURT	MAY 26		Twenty six horses evacuated from Berlin station as Railhead was closed for repairs. Cpl Cheeth sent to take over from No.3. M.Y.S. a Corporal coming to this section to take over. Nine sick horses admitted, also seven horses sent in from 2 D.A. for No.3. M.Y.S. Returns rendered	P.S.
BRUAY	27		Section moved to BRUAY. Sin sick horses left behind in charge of No. 3. M.Y.S. Two sick horses taken over and one admitted. Returns rendered.	P.S.
"	28		Pvte Brown arrived. Returns rendered. N.C.O. + men paid.	P.S.
"	29		A.V.S. made inspection. Pvte Pulling granted leave. Violet Numbrit on urgent case.	P.S.
"	30		Evacuated 138 horses from D.C.W.Y. including 129 from 47 D.A.C. Owing to this being two hours late, classification of diseases could not be checked. Cpte Puckett arrived from hospital.	P.S.
"	31		Joung horse from section posted to Units. Seven sick horses admitted, including one just evacuated from B 237/87	P.S.

SECRET

47th Division.

2

Passed please.

Joseph Abson
Major. A.V.C.
A.D.V.S. 47th Devn.

A.D.V.S.,
47th (LONDON)
DIVISION.
No. V.74
Date 5. 8. 16

To.

H.Q.
    47th London Div.

    Herewith, please
Receive War Diary of
½ London Mobile Vet. Section
for the month of July 1916.

                    Haustad
                          Capt. A.V.C.
              Cmd. ½ London M.V.S.

Vol XI

WAR DIARY
of
1/2 London Mobile Vet. Section

From 1.7.1916
To 31.7.1916.

Army Form C. 2118.

WAR DIARY
or
INTELLIGENCE SUMMARY.
(Erase heading not required.)

Instructions regarding War Diaries and Intelligence Summaries are contained in F. S. Regs., Part II. and the Staff Manual respectively. Title pages will be prepared in manuscript.

Place	Date	Hour	Summary of Events and Information	Remarks and references to Appendices
BARLIN	July 1		Twenty three sick horses admitted Evacuated. Six sick cases admitted. Returns rendered. Visited Headquarters train and inspected all horses.	
"	2		One sick horse admitted and one destroyed. Returns rendered.	
"	3		A.D.V.S. made lecture and saw the twenty one horses before evacuation also the mule sent by D.D.R. Six sick cases admitted. Visited Divisional Train.	
"	4		Ten horses for skin cases to be moved by Divisional R.E. Kit sent to B23787. Attend horse with skin grub. Twelve sick cases admitted. One sergeant returned from leave.	
"	5		A.D.V.S. provided station and attend the return of 4 Pte Clark (Smith) to Mob. Base Veterinary Stores. Three mules sent to Lechere for quantity of Maize missing. Roof of shed finished. N.C.O. men paid. One sick case admitted. Visited Divisional Train.	

T.131. Wt. W708—776. 500000. 4/15. Sir J.C.&S.

Army Form C. 2118.

WAR DIARY
or
INTELLIGENCE SUMMARY.
(Erase heading not required.)

Instructions regarding War Diaries and Intelligence Summaries are contained in F. S. Regs., Part II. and the Staff Manual respectively. Title pages will be prepared in manuscript.

Place	Date	Hour	Summary of Events and Information	Remarks and references to Appendices
BARLIN.	July 6		A.D.S. visited Section. Sick personnel admitted. Visited Field Cookies.	Jf
"	7		Thirty pack mules evacuated, seventeen of which were from 47 D.A.C. that were not at Station. Returns rendered. Sick personnel admitted.	Jf
"	8		Returns rendered. Went over to 2.2.3 Bve. followed however sleep for skin cases. completed up R.E. hut at 47 point on Dorgepeter. Sick personnel admitted.	Jf
"	9		Returns rendered. A.P.M. paid a visit to Section. Visited divisional train. Sick personnel admitted.	Jf
"	10		A.D.V.S. paid a visit to Section and arranged party to proceed to the Station and collect four Remounts. Unit to apply at Section for same.	Jf
"	11		Forty two sick horses evacuated and six enteric admitted. R.E. Officer paid visit to see how much material was required to convert hut into stanstalls.	Jf

Army Form C. 2118.

WAR DIARY
or
INTELLIGENCE SUMMARY.
(Erase heading not required.)

Instructions regarding War Diaries and Intelligence Summaries are contained in F.S. Regs., Part II. and the Staff Manual respectively. Title pages will be prepared in manuscript.

Place	Date	Hour	Summary of Events and Information	Remarks and references to Appendices
BARLIN	July 12		Staff went to lines of 9 Batts. Lond Reg. Brollet horse with spirits of joint. Nine sick evac admitted.	JP
"	13		Seven sick evac sent in to station ambs note asking for reinforcements. Sent reinforcements supplied. Three promoted on list. 4 Lond Field Amb. and 4 D.A.C. supplied with Lint, Linder and its sockets supplied by 4 R.E. for piece of plat. Eight sick evac admitted. Visited Divisional Train.	JP
"	14		A.D.M.S. and Capt. Craig visited Section Bnk. Billing sent to and detained by 25 Lond Field Amb. Scheme of Oct completed. Twelve sick evac admitted. Returns dinner.	JP
"	15		One stretcher case admitted. Returns nursed. Visits Divisional Train.	JP
"	16		Returns rendered. A.D.M.S. visited Section. Visits M.S. at Divisional Station. Pointy. Billing evacuated to No 23 Casualty Clearing Station. Five sick evac admitted.	JP

T2134. Wt. W708—776. 500000. 4/15. Sir J. C. & S.

Army Form C. 2118.

WAR DIARY
or
INTELLIGENCE SUMMARY.
(Erase heading not required.)

Instructions regarding War Diaries and Intelligence Summaries are contained in F. S. Regs., Part II. and the Staff Manual respectively. Title pages will be prepared in manuscript.

Place	Date	Hour	Summary of Events and Information	Remarks and references to Appendices
	July			
BARLIN	17		Thirty eight sick horses evacuated. Visited A.D.V.S. A.D.V.S. of R.A.D. Visited section. Eighteen sick horses admitted.	JP
"	18		R.A.D. Mobile Vet. Section entered sick & occupied by this Section. One sick case admitted.	JP
FRESNICOURT	19		Section moved to FRESNICOURT and took over from No. 3 M.V.S. Fifteen sick cases. Six more admitted.	JP
"	20		Sixteen sick horses of 2 Div. evacuated. Visited Barlin & Hill 6. Visited 4 Corps H.R. also 2 Co. Park. also A.D.C. at Barlin in evening. A.D.V.S. visited section. Six sick cases admitted.	JP
"	21		Returns rendered. Visited A.D.V.S. also 2 Co. Park. Gen Pigou visited Section and strongly approved his work that his charges suffering from mange should not be evacuated. Four sick cases admitted.	JP

WAR DIARY
or
INTELLIGENCE SUMMARY.
(Erase heading not required.)

Army Form C. 2118.

Place	Date	Hour	Summary of Events and Information	Remarks and references to Appendices
FRESNICOURT	July 22		Returns rendered. Light sick parade admitted. Visited #1 Corps H.Q.	
"	23		A.D.M.S. visited station and was informed of Genl. Supries visit. Returns rendered. Three sick parades admitted.	
"	24		D.D.R., D.D.V.S. A.D.A.M.S. & Staff Capt. visited Station. Two sick parades admitted. Twenty five sick parade admitted and evacuated. Station horse died.	
"	25		Another sick parade evacuated. Sir pick horse admitted. P.M. on horse that died. ruptured intestine. Visited A.D.V.S. re matter.	
"	26		A.D.V.S. & A.D.M.S. visited Station. V.O. from H.Q. & Corps also A.D.V.S. 37 I.D. visited Station and inspected Horse Lines. Tenders on 25th inst.	
"	27		A.D.V.S. visited Station. Heat sent to 24 Batt. Collect a mule. P.C. 25 M.V.S. visited Station. Sir pick parade admitted. Kits and men paid.	

Army Form C. 2118.

WAR DIARY
or
INTELLIGENCE SUMMARY.
(Erase heading not required.)

Instructions regarding War Diaries and Intelligence Summaries are contained in F.S. Regs., Part II. and the Staff Manual respectively. Title pages will be prepared in manuscript.

Place	Date	Hour	Summary of Events and Information	Remarks and references to Appendices
	July			
Lá THEOLOVE	28		Section moved to Theolove. Twenty nine sick horses handed over to No 2 F.M.V.S. Rations of which retained that evening. Visited No 3 & AVC also A.V.I.S.	gg
"	29		Two animals collected from Brunel Station. Sine sick horses admitted. Surplus stores sent to Guisigny	gg
"	30		Section moved to Thouro Park. Lilbury returned from Base A.V.I.S. visited Section	dg
"	31		Lieut Ray posted to H.Q. Comp Sec. Grain A.V.I.S. visited Section	dg

Vol 12

Confidential.

WAR DIARY

of

1/2 London Mobile Veterinary Section.

47th London Div.

From 1.5.16 to 31.5.16.

Army Form C. 2118.

WAR DIARY

of

INTELLIGENCE SUMMARY.

(Erase heading not required.)

Instructions regarding War Diaries and Intelligence Summaries are contained in F. S. Regs., Part II. and the Staff Manual respectively. Title pages will be prepared in manuscript.

Place	Date	Hour	Summary of Events and Information	Remarks and references to Appendices
	August			
FROHEN le GRAND	1		Section moved to FROHEN-le-GRAND.	J.G.
"	2		Returns rendered for remounts received during previous month.	J.G.
"	3		A.D.V.S. visited Section and gave directions to collect horses left behind by 21 D.A.C. Capt. Gray called and was shown two motors, five frames only being obtained for carcases. One horse unable to travel left with mayor. Sergt. Coy despatched to No.2 Veterinary Hospital. Seven sick cases admitted. T.O. 140 Sgt. Rae called to see if he could obtain two remounts.	J.G.
YVRENCH	4		Section moved to YVRENCH. No pits allotted. Temporary lines erected in open field.	J.G.
"	5		Section moved to more suitable site where excellent shelter was found. A.D.V.S. visited Section.	J.G.
			Returns rendered.	
"	6		A.D.V.S. visited Section. Two sick cases admitted. Returns rendered.	J.G.
"	7		Nineteen sick cases evacuated. A.D.V.S. visited Section. Thirteen sick cases admitted.	J.G.
"	7		Section rested. Horses greatly worried by war flies - especially afternoon.	J.G.

Army Form C. 2118.

WAR DIARY
of
INTELLIGENCE SUMMARY.
(Erase heading not required.)

Instructions regarding War Diaries and Intelligence Summaries are contained in F. S. Regs., Part II. and the Staff Manual respectively. Title pages will be prepared in manuscript.

Place	Date	Hour	Summary of Events and Information	Remarks and references to Appendices
YVRENCH	August 9		A.E. accompanied by two N.Co. visited No 22 (Base Veterinary Hospital. No complaints or suggestions made re horses evacuated. Visited No 4. Co. Train.	L
"	10		Section Routine	JL
"	11		Return march. Two horses left behind by the Artillery collected by foot. N.Co. and two visited the	JL
"	12		Fair. Sub. Billing retired section from No 3. Base Vet. Hospital. Two horses collected one by foot, other sent to march. Return march. D.A.Q.M.G. visited section to make arrangements for section treatment amount.	JL
"	13		One N.Co. and orderlies now taken by lorry to VIGNACOURT to collect A1 Remounts. R.V.S. and D.A.Q.M.G. issued icemounts to various units. Visited No 1. Co A.S.C. at ALBERT. Return march.	JL
"	14		R.V.S. visited section and started inspection of the horses which were supplied. Visited R.E. and others in remount area for examination. Eight sick were admitted. Orders received to march in morning.	JL
"	15		Section moved to NEUF-MOULIN. The site allotted was almost under water. No available pits per hand with billets for men.	JL

Army Form C. 2118.

WAR DIARY
~~INTELLIGENCE~~ SUMMARY.
(Erase heading not required.)

Instructions regarding War Diaries and Intelligence Summaries are contained in F. S. Regs., Part II. and the Staff Manual respectively. Title pages will be prepared in manuscript.

Place	Date	Hour	Summary of Events and Information	Remarks and references to Appendices
NEUF MOULIN	August 16		Ten sick cases evacuated by road to ABBEVILLE. Three sick cases admitted. A.D.V.S. visited Section.	M.
"	17		In company with A.D.V.S. visited R.E.O. A.D.V.S. visited Section. Visited Remount Depot in afternoon.	J.G.
"	18		Returns rendered A.D.V.S. visited Section. Visited No 22 Base Veterinary Hospital. Also Remount Depot. Three sick cases admitted.	J.G.
"	19		Eight sick cases evacuated by road to ABBEVILLE, including one destination. Hoel sent to lines of F.C./L. to take horse to No 22 Base Veterinary Hospital. Re-accompanied A.D. sick horse. A.D.V.S. visited Section. Returns rendered.	J.D.
"	20		Section march to AILLY-le-HAUT-CLOCHER. Returns rendered.	J.G.
"	21		" " VIGNACOURT.	J.G.
"	22		" " BAIZIEUX.	J.G.
BAIZIEUX	23		A.D.V.S. visited Section. Went by Car to meet Artillery Waggon Lines, also lines of No.1 G.A.S.C. at ALBERT.	J.G.

Army Form C. 2118.

WAR DIARY
or
INTELLIGENCE SUMMARY.
(Erase heading not required.)

Instructions regarding War Diaries and Intelligence Summaries are contained in F. S. Regs., Part II. and the Staff Manual respectively. Title pages will be prepared in manuscript.

Place	Date	Hour	Summary of Events and Information	Remarks and references to Appendices
BAIZIEUX	August 24		II D.V.S. & Army with A.D.V.S. visited section and inspected section horses. Visited Artillery waggon lines. Three sick horses admitted.	J.S.
"	25		Have received sitting position and times of artillery. Visited No 2 & No 3 A.D.S. visited Section. Also Capt. Craig and Bricken. N.Co. and new pair. Returns rendered. Three sick horses admitted.	J.S.
"	26		Returns rendered. Lt. Christie taken ill, visited by D.A.D.M.S. who ordered his removal by ambulance to No 6. Field Amb. Three sick horses admitted. Heavy rain caused horse standings to become very muddy.	J.S.
"	27		Visited Camp Com. and Town Major and received permission to move section to another site. Horses put under cover and new site hilled in slurry. Returns rendered. Two sick horses admitted.	J.S.
"	28		A.D.V.S. visited section, also Camp Com. to make arrangements for charges of H.Q. to be placed under notice with section horses owing to continuous heavy rain. One horse destroyed and buried.	J.S.

T2134. Wt. W708—776. 500000. 4/15. Sr. J. C. & S.

Army Form C. 2118.

WAR DIARY
INTELLIGENCE SUMMARY.
(Erase heading not required.)

Instructions regarding War Diaries and Intelligence Summaries are contained in F. S. Regs., Part II. and the Staff Manual respectively. Title pages will be prepared in manuscript.

Place	Date	Hour	Summary of Events and Information	Remarks and references to Appendices
	AUGUST			
BAIZIEUX	29		Sen sick horses evacuated to No.7 Veterinary Hospital. A.D.V.S. visited Section. Seven sick cases admitted. Very heavy rain almost flooded horse standings.	S.
"	30		D.D.V.R. visited Section with A.D.V.S. and post five horses. Capt. Townend visited Section. Six cases admitted. Visited D.A.C., "N" Bty. R.H.A. also H.Q. 2nd. Cav. Corps.	S.
"	31		Visited H.Q. 2nd. Cav. Corps. Returns rendered. Twelve sick cases admitted.	S.

[signature]
Capt.

MOBILE VETERINARY SECTION
½ London
4.10.16
47th LONDON DIVISION

To.
H.Q.
47th London Div.

Herewith, please receive,
Original Copy of War Diary of
this Section, for the month
ending 30. 9. 16.

Houston(?)
Capt. A.V.C.
Cmd. ½ London M.V.S.
47th London Div.

CONFIDENTIAL   Vol 13

WAR DIARY

of

½ London Mobile Veterinary Section
47th London Div.

From 1. 9. 16
To 30. 9. 16

Army Form C. 2118.

WAR DIARY
or
INTELLIGENCE SUMMARY.
(Erase heading not required.)

Instructions regarding War Diaries and Intelligence Summaries are contained in F. S. Regs., Part II. and the Staff Manual respectively. Title pages will be prepared in manuscript.

MOBILE VETERINARY SECTION
47th LONDON DIVISION
1.9.16

Place	Date	Hour	Summary of Events and Information	Remarks and references to Appendices
BAIZIEUX	Sept 1		Twenty four sick horses evacuated from FRESNICOURT. Detachment to collect sick horses from lines of 2/3 R.E. also 1/o Bde. R.F.A. Charger from H.Q. sent into section with suspected colic. Visited by Staff Officers also O.R.E. three sick. Returnerenies	
"	2		Returns received. D.A.V.M.G. visited section. One sick horse admitted. P.M. held on horse from H.Q. — Cause of death Volvulus.	
"	3		Visited III Corps H.Q. and inspected horses. A.P.M. visited section also Capt Ryan. Six sick cases admitted. Returnerenies	
"	4		One sick case admitted. A.D.V.S. visited section	
"	5		War diary fol. Previous month sent to H.Q. Nine sick cases admitted	
"	6		One sick case admitted	

Army Form C. 2118.

WAR DIARY
of
INTELLIGENCE SUMMARY.
(Erase heading not required.)

Instructions regarding War Diaries and Intelligence Summaries are contained in F. S. Regs., Part II. and the Staff Manual respectively. Title pages will be prepared in manuscript.

Place	Date	Hour	Summary of Events and Information	Remarks and references to Appendices
BAIZIEUX	Sept 7		Three sick cases admitted. O.Cos and men paid.	J.S.
"	8		Many friends of Grant at St Albans in aid of A.Y.C. funds - subscribed to N.Cos and men. Capt. Craig visited Section. Two sick cases admitted. Returns rendered	J.S.
"	9		Ten sick cases evacuated. Orders received to move on following Monday. One sick case admitted. Returns rendered.	J.S.
"	10		Six sick cases admitted. Backs seen today on motor. Secret orders received. Returns rendered.	J.S.
"	11		Section march to ALBERT. Three sick cases admitted.	J.S.
ALBERT	12		Comp. Com. in company with A.D.V.S. visited Section and inspected lines. A.P.M. visited Section in afternoon. Visited No. 2 C. A.S.C. and inspected all horses. Two sick cases admitted	J.S.

T2134. Wt. W708—776. 500000. 4/15. Sir J. C. & S.

WAR DIARY
or
INTELLIGENCE SUMMARY.

Army Form C. 2118.

Place	Date	Hour	Summary of Events and Information	Remarks and references to Appendices
ALBERT	13		A.V.S. & Corp. Com. visited Section & was shopped from H.Q. Hrs had resigned to some injury to shoulder. Two cases received from No.2 M.V.S. that were under orders for move	J.S.
"	14		Fourteen sick cases evacuated. One horse sent to Bus-les M.V.S. for evacuation. Four sick cases admitted.	R.S.
"	15		Pick bulling horses no reinforcement. Visited lines of C235 Bty. and inspected horses. Visited R.T.O. and made arrangements for evacuation. Three sick cases admitted neighbourhood to lines visited. Capt Gray visits Section. Returns rendered.	J.S.
"	16		Fifteen sick horses evacuated. Horse sent to C235 Bty. to collect animal there. He was fetched from M.V.S. 14 Div. A.V.S. visits Section. Corps officer Veterinary cases admitted. Returns rendered.	J.S.
"	17		Horse sent to Dieppe to collect sick horse. A.V.S. visits Section. Corps officer. Seven sick cases admitted. Returns rendered.	J.S.

WAR DIARY
INTELLIGENCE SUMMARY.
(Erase heading not required.)

Army Form C. 2118.

Place	Date	Hour	Summary of Events and Information	Remarks and references to Appendices
ALBERT	SEPTER 18		Heavy rain. Nine other fourteen sick cases admitted. A.D.V.S. visited station	H.S.
"	19		Twenty four sick cases admitted. Shot from Guards M.V.S. I think more float cases to station. Sir cases shell wounds collected from lines of C103 Bty. Remounted by float. Visited C103 Bty also 17th Battn lines to see wounded horses, also C.C. Station at MEAULTE re evacuations. Six pick cases admitted	J.S.
"	20		Six wounded horses evacuated. A.D.V.S. visited Station. Sgt. Mowatt + Latham sent to C.C.S.	J.S.
"	21		Visited all companies of R.E. and inspected horses. Returns rendered.	J.S.
"	22		A.D.V.S. visited Station, also A.D.V.S. 1 Div. re horses with abscess on shoulder. Horse operated on. Seven pick cases admitted. Visited Field Cashier. NCO + two rank. Sick were cases evacuated to C.C.S. Returns rendered.	J.S.

WAR DIARY

INTELLIGENCE SUMMARY

Army Form C. 2118.

(Erase heading not required.)

Place	Date	Hour	Summary of Events and Information	Remarks and references to Appendices
ALBERT	SEPTR 23		Went out to Johnson Field Amb. A.D.Y.S. D.H. visited section visited MAMETZ WOOD and inspected flat case of T.236.Bty. NCO was posted Baths at ALBERT. Returns rendered. Two sick cases admitted.	
"	24		L.A. QUATRO M.Y.S. visited section to report one O.R. for inoculation. Seven sick cases admitted. Returns rendered.	
"	25		Twelve sick cases evacuated to MEAULTE. Nine sick cases admitted. One O.R. returned from C.C.S. and Pvte. Motley to take his place.	
"	26		A.D.Y.S. visited section and tried man reported for inoculation. Went out to lines of T.236.Bty. to collect sick horse. One horse destroyed with open shallow front fetlock bursa. Nine sick cases admitted.	
"	27		Thirteen sick cases evacuated to C.C.S. Three sick cases admitted.	

WAR DIARY

INTELLIGENCE SUMMARY.
(Erase heading not required.)

Army Form C. 2118.

Instructions regarding War Diaries and Intelligence Summaries are contained in F. S. Regs., Part II. and the Staff Manual respectively. Title pages will be prepared in manuscript.

Place	Date	Hour	Summary of Events and Information	Remarks and references to Appendices
ALBERT	SEPT 28		Heat pent to line of 6 Batt. Kerllies pulvulo horse with punctured foot. Sin sick cases admitted. One section horse sick.	
"	29		P.M. held on horse that died previous night. Cause of death tetanus. Corpse burnt. Two sick cases admitted. A.D.V.S., A.P.M. & Capt Craig visited Section. Four sick cases admitted.	
"	30		Two sick cases floated. Visited for evacuation. A.D.V.S. visited Section and ordered all evacuated horses to be marked with number of Section. One sick case admitted.	

[Stamp: MOBILE VETERINARY SECTION / ½ London / 5.11.16 / 47th LONDON DIVISION]

To.
A.D.V.S.
    47th London Div.

    Herewith please receive War Diary for this Section, for the month ending 31.10.16.

                           [Signature]
                              Capt. A.V.C.
                    Cmd. ½ London M.V.S.
                      47th London Div.

Confidential.

Vol 14

WAR DIARY
of
1/2 London Mobile Vet. Section
47th London Div.

From. 1.10.16
To. 31. 10. 16

Army Form C. 2118.

WAR DIARY
or
INTELLIGENCE SUMMARY
(Erase heading not required.)

Instructions regarding War Diaries and Intelligence Summaries are contained in F. S. Regs., Part II. and the Staff Manual respectively. Title Pages will be prepared in manuscript.

Place	Date	Hour	Summary of Events and Information	Remarks and references to Appendices
	Oct.			
ALBERT	1		A.D.S. visited section, re proposed visit by D.D.R. and left particulars of horses the Capt. A.P.M. Capt Phipps & Lt Lucas visited section. Returns rendered. Four sick cases admitted.	J.P.
"	2		D.D.R. visited section and inspected horses. Visited lines of 18 Batt. trans horses & had them groomed by public, two to be moved by their A.D.V.S. visited section. One sick case admitted.	J.P.
"	3		Thirty six cases evacuated including seven remount cases from 15 Corps M.T. Brat sent to lines of 18 Batt and removed two cases. Twenty two cases admitted.	J.P.
"	4		A.D.V.S. visited section and went with O.C. to select a new site for section.	J.P.
"	5		Section moved to FRICOURT. A.D.V.S. visited section. Ten sick cases admitted.	J.P.
FRICOURT	6		Stallion visited for men, forage and harness. Eight sick cases admitted. A.D.V.S. visited section. Returns rendered. M Corken pain.	J.P.

Army Form C. 2118.

WAR DIARY
INTELLIGENCE SUMMARY
(Erase heading not required.)

Instructions regarding War Diaries and Intelligence Summaries are contained in F. S. Regs., Part II. and the Staff Manual respectively. Title Pages will be prepared in manuscript.

Place	Date	Hour	Summary of Events and Information	Remarks and references to Appendices
FRICOURT.	Oct. 7		Returns rendered. Visited ALBERT. Made arrangements for evacuation of horses. Twenty six sick cases admitted.	J.S.
	8		Thirty three sick cases evacuated from ALBERT including two cases by float. One remount collected from station. Capt. Chapman visited station and reported that this remount horse left with D.A.C. he collected. Visited A.D.V.S. also O.C. M.V.S. 12 D.V. also ALBERT stores. Returns rendered.	J.S.
"	9		A.D.V.S. visited station and left orders for moving on horses. Sick cases sent to M.V.S. 12 D.V. and arrangements made to find cases for evacuation to this M.V.S. 1 O.R. 15 troops provided section. Fourteen sick cases admitted and one destroyed rendered.	J.S.
"	10		Sick horses evacuated to 12 D.V. M.V.S. One N.C.O. and three men left behind with D.A.C. 1 from reserves arriving and receiving post. Section moved to BAIZIEUX. Visited No 3 C. A.O.C. Three sick cases admitted. A.D.V.S. visited Station.	J.S.

Army Form C. 2118.

WAR DIARY
INTELLIGENCE SUMMARY
(Erase heading not required.)

Instructions regarding War Diaries and Intelligence Summaries are contained in F. S. Regs., Part II. and the Staff Manual respectively. Title Pages will be prepared in manuscript.

Place	Date	Hour	Summary of Events and Information	Remarks and references to Appendices
BAIZIEUX	Oct. 11		A.D.V.S. posted section and gave orders for move on following friday. Visits R.T.O. & R.S.O. FRESHENCOURT re execution of orders. Sick parade to 42 b.m.b. to collect horses. Sick cases admitted, including one found.	J.S.
"	12		Eight sick cases admitted and evacuated. Visits No 3 C.A.S.C. also M.V.S. Northumbrian Div. Four sick cases sent to M.V.S. 50 Div. A.D.V.S. posted section. N.Co. men from nominal nursing post rejoined section.	J.S.
St SAUVIER	13		Section moved to St SAUVIER and with the night. Six remounts handed over by A.D.V.S. on the march. Returns rendered.	J.S.
FAUCOURT	14		Sick continued to FAUCOURT. Billets found for men. One sick case admitted. Returns rendered.	J.S.
"	15		Three sick cases evacuated by train to No. 22. Vet Hospital. Visited No. 2. Car Remount Depot. Cotenement pairs received. Returns rendered.	J.S.

Army Form C. 2118.

WAR DIARY
INTELLIGENCE SUMMARY
(Erase heading not required.)

Place	Date	Hour	Summary of Events and Information	Remarks and references to Appendices
FAUCOURT	Oct" 16		Visited No. 2 Adv. Remount Depot and collected charges of 66 Foots. Preparation made for entraining	J.S.
"	17		Entrained at PONT REMY. Arrived 10.30 p.m., entrained 4.30 p.m.	J.S.
"	18		Arrived at GODEWAERSVELDE Station 2.0 a.m., detrained and travelled beside road HOOGRAFE.	J.S.
SHEET 27. L 29 q 7.4	19		Orders for evacuation received from D.D.V.S. 2 ARMY. Headquarters to Godewaersvelde Station. Field Hospital. Visited No.2 & No.3 Co. A.S.C. Visited Field Cashier.	J.S.
"	20		A.P.V.S. visited Section. Visited No.2, 3, 4, Co. A.S.C. N.C.O & men paid. Returns rendered.	J.S.
"	21		O.C. began sent to R.E. dump for material to cover place for horses. Veterinary stores left behind when on trek sent for. Two men sick sent to No. 1. A.V.C. when sick cases admitted. Returns rendered.	J.S.

Army Form C. 2118.

WAR DIARY
INTELLIGENCE SUMMARY
(Erase heading not required.)

Instructions regarding War Diaries and Intelligence Summaries are contained in F. S. Regs., Part II. and the Staff Manual respectively. Title Pages will be prepared in manuscript.

MOBILE VETERINARY SECTION
47th LONDON DIVISION

Place	Date	Hour	Summary of Events and Information	Remarks and references to Appendices
SHEET 27 L29 a 7.4	Octr. 22		A.D.V.S. visited section also Capt. Craig. Visited A.S.C. & 523 Bty. and made arrangements for collecting all the horses in this battery. Commenced setting of shed. Returns prepared. One man detained in field ambulance.	J.S.
"	23		Visited 523 Bty. and maintained 152 horses and 24 mules. Visited C.L D. Amb. and inspected all horses. Eleven sick cases admitted.	J.S.
"	24		Adj. from E.R.E. visited section re material for shed. Material collected from R.E. dump. Capt. Craig visited section and requested floors to remove manure. Horse pit cases admitted.	J.S.
"	25		Visited D.D.V.S. office at HAZEBROUCK re evacuation of sick horses by special train. Went round to collect horses. Twenty three sick cases admitted.	J.S.
"	26		Special train load of horses evacuated to NEUFCHATEL, 99 from Johnson M.V.S. 53 from 52 M.V.S. 47 from 41 M.V.S. O.C. 42 London M.V.S. in charge of horses. Two sick cases admitted.	J.S.

Army Form C. 2118.

WAR DIARY
INTELLIGENCE SUMMARY
(Erase heading not required.)

Instructions regarding War Diaries and Intelligence Summaries are contained in F. S. Regs., Part II. and the Staff Manual respectively. Title Pages will be prepared in manuscript.

Place	Date	Hour	Summary of Events and Information	Remarks and references to Appendices
SHEET 27 L29 d.7.4	Oct. 27		Returned from NEUFCHATEL. Capt Bryan visited section and left car of horse which was sick from suspected anthrax. Two sick cases admitted. Returns rendered.	J.S.
"	28		On examination microscopically, with negative result. Visited A.D.V.S. also No 1, 2, 3 & 4 C. A.S.C. also 523 Bty. Returns rendered. Eight sick cases admitted.	J.S.
"	29		A.V.S. visited section, visited 523 Bty. Horses sent to collect horses from C.235 Bty & 2 L Field Amb. One horse discharged from Field Amb and rejoined section. Two sick cases admitted. Returns rendered.	J.S.
"	30		Visited 523 Bty and injected picric acid cases suffering from pneumonia with formalin solution. Visited A.S.C. all companies.	J.S.
"	31		Visited A.D.V.S. 523 Bty, also No. 4. Co A.S.C. Four pick cases admitted.	J.S.

John Southail
Capt M.C. (TF)
Cmd 1/2 London M.V.S.
47th London Div

MOBILE VETERINARY SECTION
No. 1/2 London
Date 5.12.16
47th LONDON DIVISION

To.
H.Q.
47th London Div.

Herewith, please receive, war diary of this section for the month ending 30.11.16.

J. Laurhach
Capt. A.V.C.
Cmd. 1/2 London M.V.S.
47th London Div.

"A.D.V.S."
47th (LONDON)
DIVISION.
No............
Date............

Confidential Vol 15

WAR DIARY
of
½ London Mobile Veterinary Section

From 1. 11. 1916
To 30. 11. 1916

Army Form C. 2118.

WAR DIARY
INTELLIGENCE SUMMARY
(Erase heading not required.)

Instructions regarding War Diaries and Intelligence Summaries are contained in F. S. Regs., Part II. and the Staff Manual respectively. Title Pages will be prepared in manuscript.

Place	Date	Hour	Summary of Events and Information	Remarks and references to Appendices
SHEET 24 L29a7.5.	NOV. 1		Wired O.A.V.S. to obtain particulars of horses to be evacuated on morrow. One sick case admitted.	J.S.
"	2		One hundred and only two sick horses evacuated by special train to base A.V.S. mobile Section. Achille trumpets to be shot, sent to pass. Two sick cases admitted.	J.S.
"	3		Returns rendered. Four sick cases admitted.	J.S.
"	4		Returns rendered. Two sick cases admitted, one from A.23.Bty suffering from sand colic, died as soon as it reached section.	J.S.
"	5		Carcase of horse buried, difficulty experienced with water when digging grave. One sick case admitted. Returns rendered.	J.S.
"	6		N.C.O's & men paid. Twelve sick cases admitted.	J.S.

WAR DIARY

INTELLIGENCE SUMMARY

Army Form C. 2118.

Place	Date	Hour	Summary of Events and Information	Remarks and references to Appendices
SHEET 21 k.29.a.75.	Nov. 7		Twenty pair pick horses admitted. Visited A.O.C. No.1 & 2. Companies, also 523 Bty.	J.S.
"	8		Visited A.O.C. No.3 & 4. Company. Twelve pick horses admitted. Visited 523 Bty.	J.S.
"	9		Went and taken of 14 trees. C. R.E. trestles, horses with knop taken back. Timber fetched from R.E. dump to continue roof of shed. Four pick cases admitted.	J.S.
"	10		Returns rendered. One pick case admitted. Visited A.V.C.	J.S.
"	11		Went out to lines of 141 Bde. M.G. Co. Orders received to send forage cart to station to collect Stenatello from remounts. Stenatello retained as remount but over at C.R.A. Adjt. S. Visited Station. Three pick cases admitted. Pole Roll. One admitted to hospital. Returns rendered.	J.S.
"	12		Eighty pick horses evacuated by special train. Visited A.O.C. & 523 Bty. and reported to K.A.B.T.S. in evening. Two pick cases admitted. Returns rendered.	J.S.

Army Form C. 2118.

WAR DIARY
or
INTELLIGENCE SUMMARY

(Erase heading not required.)

Instructions regarding War Diaries and Intelligence Summaries are contained in F. S. Regs., Part II. and the Staff Manual respectively. Title Pages will be prepared in manuscript.

Place	Date	Hour	Summary of Events and Information	Remarks and references to Appendices
SHEET 27. K.29.a.75.	Nov. 13		Sent telins of D.2.35 Bly to collect pick horse. Report forwarded on loss of microscope. A.V.S. visited section. Visited A.O.C. in afternoon and again at night to see an urgent case. Three pick cases admitted.	JS
"	14		Visited A.O.C. and found urgent case case. D.D.V.R. visited section on arrival east at horses. Nine pick cases admitted A.V.S. visited section.	JS
"	15		Four pick cases admitted.	JS
"	16		Received message to meet 6th L. Brig. Amb. to see horse. Horse died on arrival. Two horses east but D.D.V.R. sent to Sica Remount Depot by order of D.D.V.R. Ten pick cases admitted.	JS
"	17		A.V.S. visited section. F.M. Kell on horse of 6 Sica Am. Cases of Mange return'd to. Wts received from Capt Craig re horse alleged to have been sent to section and refused admission. Returns rendered.	JS

2449 Wt. W14957/Mgo 750,000 1/16 J.B.C. & A. Forms/C.2118/12.

Army Form C. 2118.

WAR DIARY
or
INTELLIGENCE SUMMARY
(Erase heading not required.)

Instructions regarding War Diaries and Intelligence Summaries are contained in F. S. Regs., Part II. and the Staff Manual respectively. Title Pages will be prepared in manuscript.

Place	Date	Hour	Summary of Events and Information	Remarks and references to Appendices
SHEET 27 L.29 d.4.5	Nov. 18		Visited A.O.C. also 523 Bty. Three sick cases admitted. Returns rendered.	JP
"	19		Thirty one sick horses examined by veterinary officer A.B.V.S. 3rd M. Corps officer visited section and inspected huts, cookhouse, picketing lines T.O. 3 Setts called to try to harness two L.D. horses. Eight cases admitted including two mules to be tested with mallein. Returns rendered.	JP
"	20		Orders received to inspect horses of X Corps Cav. and report to H.M.V.O. Horse sent to collect horse left by Australian Artillery. Six sick cases admitted. N.Cos. and men paid.	JP
"	21		Staff sent to lines of 14 Royal Welsh Fus. in morning and to #7 D.A.C. in afternoon to collect the cases of forwardness colic. A.B.V.S. visited section. Four sick cases admitted.	JP
"	22		Staff sent to X Corps Cav. to collect horse with kicked hock. Sergt. John reported to station by orders of H.Q. 536 Bde. Nine sick cases admitted. Visited A.O.C.	JP

WAR DIARY
or
INTELLIGENCE SUMMARY

Army Form C. 2118.

Place	Date	Hour	Summary of Events and Information	Remarks and references to Appendices
SHEET 27. L.29 d.7.5	NOV. 23		Vet sent to line of C.Q.T. to collect horses with infected hair. Cannot arrange isolation to collect horses from remounts - thro only period. Div sick were admitted.	
	24		A.D.V.S. with Staff Officer visited section and examined horse stands up. Visited X Corps Vet. Report sent re horses collected from Remounts. Div sick were admitted. Returns rendered	
	25		On licences and rendering sick horses evacuated by special train. P.O. S. Henderson M.R.S. and one N.C.O. in charge. Pulso Burns & Leeham journeyed in lorry. Returns rendered.	
	26		A.D.V.S. visited section and examined sick horse to be destroyed; purchase supplied. Returns rendered. Div sick were admitted. P.O. returned from evacuation of sick horses.	
	27		Visited A.V.C. Returns rendered forwarded to headquarters. Div sick cases admitted.	

Army Form C. 2118.

WAR DIARY
or
INTELLIGENCE SUMMARY
(Erase heading not required.)

Instructions regarding War Diaries and Intelligence Summaries are contained in F.S. Regs., Part II. and the Staff Manual respectively. Title Pages will be prepared in manuscript.

Place	Date	Hour	Summary of Events and Information	Remarks and references to Appendices
SHEET 27 L.29.a.7.5	Nov 28		Visited X Corps Car. and inspected horses, one to be sent into station. Capt Anderson with another officer visited station and inspected horses standing. Visited A.D.C. Two sick cases admitted. Visited C.P.S.S.H. by request of Area Comm.	J.A.
	29		A.D.V.S. and Staff Capt. visited section. Visited X Corps Car. Horse sent to line of 93 R.F. to collect an urgent case. Sgt Greenhill reported to Section. Four sick cases admitted.	J.A.
	30		Horse sent to line of 523 B4 to collect horse with kicked knee. Visited A.D.C. A.P.M. visited section. Two sick cases admitted. Return no sick.	J.A.

Montair
Capt. A.V.C.

2449 Wt. W14957/M90 750,000 1/16 J.B.C. & A. Forms/C.2118/12.

To.

H.Q.
47th London Div.

Herewith, please receive WAR DIARY for month of DECEMBER for this Section.

Southall
Capt. A.V.C.
Cmd. ½ London M.V.S.
47th London Div.

CONFIDENTIAL. Vol 16

WAR DIARY

of

1/2 London Mobile Veterinary Section
47th London Div.

From 1.12.16   To 31.12.16

Army Form C. 2118.

WAR DIARY
or
INTELLIGENCE SUMMARY

(Erase heading not required.)

Instructions regarding War Diaries and Intelligence Summaries are contained in F. S. Regs., Part II. and the Staff Manual respectively. Title Pages will be prepared in manuscript.

Place	Date	Hour	Summary of Events and Information	Remarks and references to Appendices
SHEET 24. L29.d.7.4	Dec. 1		Staff went to H.Q. X Corps Car to collect horse. Urgent message from A.D.V.S. asking for V.O. to come and stand know. Four sick cases admitted. Returns rendered.	J.S.
"	2		Returns rendered. Visited all Train Companies and inspected horses. Six sick cases admitted	J.S.
"	3		A.D.V.S. notified section leaving final instructions before proceeding to England on extended leave. Returns rendered. Six sick cases admitted.	J.S.
"	4		Duties of A.D.V.S. taken over by P.O. to known M.V.S. Dogs French officer attached Section from 140 Infy. Bde. N.C.Os. & men paid. Four sick cases admitted.	J.S.
"	5		Visited A.D.V.S. offices in morning and again in evening. Visited D.M.R. and made arrangements for three A.V.C. Sergeants departure to France. Four sick cases admitted.	J.S.

2449 Wt. W14957/M90 750,000 1/16 J.B.C. & A. Forms/C.2118/12.

Army Form C. 2118.

WAR DIARY
or
INTELLIGENCE SUMMARY

(Erase heading not required.)

Instructions regarding War Diaries and Intelligence Summaries are contained in F. S. Regs., Part II. and the Staff Manual respectively. Title Pages will be prepared in manuscript.

Place	Date	Hour	Summary of Events and Information	Remarks and references to Appendices
SHEET 21 L.29.a.4.4.	Decr 6		Visited A.D.V.S. office. Visited R.E. dump and arranged for supply of material to complete roof of shed. Visited D.H.Q. Arrange for transport of bricks from YPRES to station. Three Sergeants A.V.C. sent to No. 2 Base Vet. Hospital.	J.S.
"	7		Visited A.D.V.S. office, also No. 4 Co. A.O.C., D.H.Q. Signal Company and 6 horses Gun Park and inspected horses.	J.S.
"	8		Returns rendered. Visited A.D.V.S. office, also Signal Co. also D.H.Q. transport arrangements for transport of bricks. Visited A.S.C. all sections. Three sick cases admitted.	J.S.
"	9		Inspection casting of pit-props. Visited A.D.V.S. office. Returns rendered.	J.S.
"	10		Visited A.D.V.S. office. Limber drawn from R.E. dump. Capt. Cruickshank R.A.V.C. One sick case admitted. Returns rendered.	J.S.
"	11		Visited A.D.V.S. office, also A.S.C. Clipping machine lent to 1/4 R.W. Fus^{rs}.	J.S.

2449 Wt. W14957/M90 750,000 1/16 J.B.C. & A. Forms/C.2118/12.

WAR DIARY or INTELLIGENCE SUMMARY

Army Form C. 2118.

Place	Date	Hour	Summary of Events and Information	Remarks and references to Appendices
SHEET 27 L29.a.74.	Dec. 12		Visited A.D.V.S. offices. Enquire sent to P.R.F.S. for truck but no one available for this section. Two sick cases admitted.	J.S.
"	13		Visited A.D.V.S. offices. Forty six sick cases evacuated by special train. Six sick cases admitted.	J.S.
"	14		Visited A.D.V.S. offices, D.H.Q. and Signal Camp and inspected all horses. One O.R. Pte MARTIN posted to this section. Two sick cases admitted.	J.S.
"	15		Visited A.D.V.S. offices. Went out to B235 Bty to collect horse with badly broken knees. Return received. Three sick cases admitted.	J.S.
"	16		Visited A.D.V.S. offices. Court of Enquiry held at H.Q. Div Train to investigate the loss of microscope in possession of this section. O.C. and other witnesses attended and gave evidence. Enquiry adjourned. Sick horses collected from R.E. dump. Return received.	J.S.

Army Form C. 2118.

WAR DIARY
or
INTELLIGENCE SUMMARY

(Erase heading not required.)

Instructions regarding War Diaries and Intelligence Summaries are contained in F. S. Regs., Part II. and the Staff Manual respectively. Title Pages will be prepared in manuscript.

Place	Date	Hour	Summary of Events and Information	Remarks and references to Appendices
SHEET 21 L29d.7.4.	Dec. 17		Visited A.D.V.S. office. Horse with broken knees destroyed and carcase buried. Lines sent for sheets to YPRES, now available for the section. One sick case admitted. Returns rendered.	J.S.
"	18		Sent out to H.Q. X Corps Cav. Tractor Horse. Surplus Vet. Medical and E. to No. 2 Base Vet. Stores. Visited A.D.V.S. office. Sent EAMES evacuated sick. N.Cos & men paid. Three sick cases admitted.	J.S.
"	19		Visited A.D.V.S. office also D.H.Q. and four companies of F.S.C. Papers received asking for further witnesses for Court of Enquiry on loss of the messages. One sick case admitted.	J.S.
"	20		Sent out to H.Q. X Corps Cav. Tractor horse. Capt. Craig made lect. on treat. on outbreak of influenza in 142 Inf. Bde. Lieut Garment proceeded on leave, also Pte. Tilbury granted special leave. Three sick cases admitted.	J.S.

Army Form C. 2118.

WAR DIARY
or
INTELLIGENCE SUMMARY
(Erase heading not required.)

Instructions regarding War Diaries and Intelligence Summaries are contained in F. S. Regs., Part II. and the Staff Manual respectively. Title Pages will be prepared in manuscript.

Place	Date	Hour	Summary of Events and Information	Remarks and references to Appendices
SHEET 27. L29a74.	Dec. 21		Visited A.D.V.S. office. Loading party sent to YPRES to collect two lorry loads of bricks. Visited all companies of F.A.C. Sick cases admitted	J.B.
"	22		Returns rendered. Visited A.D.V.S. office. One sick case admitted	J.B.
"	23		Sent pair to №236 By. to collect horses with punctured sole. Visited O.D.M.S. office also D.H.R. and Signal Corps. Wind blew roof off shed and damaged mens' huts. Three were cases admitted. Returns rendered.	J.B.
"	24		Visited A.D.V.S. office. Stray mule sent into station. Loading party sent to YPRES to collect two lorry loads of bricks. Returns rendered.	
"	25		Visited A.D.V.S. office. Capts. Bryden & Shaeth visited section and remained for dinner. O.C. present at dinner.	J.B.
"	26		Visited A.D.V.S. office. Saw all companies of A.C. Inspected all horses.	

WAR DIARY
or
INTELLIGENCE SUMMARY

(Erase heading not required.)

Army Form C. 2118.

Instructions regarding War Diaries and Intelligence Summaries are contained in F. S. Regs., Part II. and the Staff Manual respectively. Title Pages will be prepared in manuscript.

Place	Date	Hour	Summary of Events and Information	Remarks and references to Appendices
SHEET 27 L.29.d.7.2.	Dec 28		Visited A.D.V.S. office. also I.W.R. and Signal Company. One pick case admitted.	J.S.
	29		Visited A.S.V.S. office. Two Staff officers visited section and inspected standings in field. Eight pick cases admitted. Visited all companies of 7.D.C.	J.S.
			Sent sick to D.A.C. & called mule suffering from acute shell wounds. Knacking party sent to YPRES for disease. One pick case admitted. Returns rendered. Visited A.D.V.S. office in morning and again in evening.	J.S.
	30		Sent sent to Cape Belge to collect badly wounded horse of 34 Bty. Returns rendered. Visited A.S.V.S. office - also I.H.R. and Signal Co. Give pick cases admitted	J.S.
	31		Sent sent to collect two badly wounded horses of 34 Bty. Visited 9 D.V.S. office also all companies of Div Train. Returns rendered. Five pick cases admitted.	J.S.

Mackay
Capt. R.C.

To.

H.Q
47th London Div.

Herewith please find
WAR DIARY for this Section for
the month ending 31. 1. 1917.

Nouthall
Capt. A.V.C.
Cmd. 1/2 London M.V.S
47th London Div.

CONFIDENTIAL

WAR DIARY Vol.17

of

1/London Mobile Veterinary Section
47th London Div.

From 1.1.17
To 31.1.17

Army Form C. 2118.

WAR DIARY
INTELLIGENCE SUMMARY
(Erase heading not required.)

Instructions regarding War Diaries and Intelligence Summaries are contained in F. S. Regs., Part II. and the Staff Manual respectively. Title Pages will be prepared in manuscript.

MOBILE VETERINARY SECTION
No. ....
Date. 1/1/17
47th LONDON DIVISION

Place	Date	Hour	Summary of Events and Information	Remarks and references to Appendices
SHEET 24. L.20.a.7.4.	JAN. 1.		Visited A.D.V.S. office. also Field Cashier. Two O.R. returned from leave. Two O.R. and men paid. Two sick horses admitted. Returns rendered	f.s.
"	2		Visited A.D.V.S. office and also lines of A.S.C. Two sick horses admitted.	f.s.
"	3		Visited A.D.V.S. office also lines of 6th London Field Amb. and inspected all horses. Six sick horses admitted.	f.s.
"	4		Visited A.D.V.S. office. Sgt sent to 140 Bde Signal Co. to collect charges also to H.Q. wing. Pte hedger charges. Fifty four horses evacuated by road to St Omer. Sheep caught resting rations and taken to A.F.M.	f.s.
"	5		Visited A.D.V.S. office. Returns rendered. Water ambulance space and stained horses. Two picrns horses taken in float to Mob. Ambulance for evacuation.	f.s.

WAR DIARY
INTELLIGENCE SUMMARY
(Erase heading not required.)

Army Form C. 2118.

Place	Date	Hour	Summary of Events and Information	Remarks and references to Appendices
SHEET 27. JAN.				
K.29.d.7.4	6		Visited A.D.V.S. office. Four sick cases admitted. Returns rendered.	
"	7		Visited A.D.V.S. office. Party returned from evacuation of horses and reported one horse destroyed for fractured tibia. One man kicked and hospitalized. Sick returns in hospital. Returns rendered. Twelve sick cases admitted.	
"	8		Visited A.D.V.S. office. ONE man evacuated sick. Horse sent to lines of C236 B4. to collect wounded horse. THREE stray horses sent to Field Remount Section B.E.F. orders of D.D.R. Visited all companies of R.A.S.C. Three sick cases admitted.	
"	9		Visited A.D.V.S. office. Horse taken to X Corps workshops for repair. One sick case admitted.	
"	10		Visited A.D.V.S. office. Trains received to inspect remounts due tomorrow in evening. Visited three sections of D.A.C. also II 238 Bty. and inspected horses for skin disease. Seven sick cases rendered to this section.	

Army Form C. 2118.

WAR DIARY
or
INTELLIGENCE SUMMARY
(Erase heading not required.)

Instructions regarding War Diaries and Intelligence Summaries are contained in F. S. Regs., Part II. and the Staff Manual respectively. Title Pages will be prepared in manuscript.

MOBILE VETERINARY SECTION
No. ...
Date ...
47th LONDON DIVISION

Place	Date	Hour	Summary of Events and Information	Remarks and references to Appendices
SHEET 27. N29 a.7.5	JAN. 11		Remounts which arrived during the night issued from Mob Vet. D.A.C. Visited A.V.T.S. office also No. 3 Co. A.S.C. and spent some hrs this evening with the duties. Visited Signal Co. and Field P.M. on horse that died suddenly.	JS
"	12		Visited No. Twenty two sick cases evacuated helpless. seven cases admitted. Visited A.D.V.S. office. Two loan Officers supplied by A.S.C. Two cases admitted. Returns rendered	JS
"	13		Visited A.D.V.S. office. Also all Companies of A.S.C. and Field Amb. Thirteen sick cases admitted	JS
"	14		Visited A.V.T.S. office. Horse hoppered from 2/3 Bgd. M.T.S. Three urgent cases to Mob Amb. for examination. One may discharged from hospital. Balance admitted.	JS
"	15		Visited A.V.T.S. office. Also Field Bakery. Two cases evacuated by Mob Amb. NCO and men paid. Nine sick cases admitted.	JS
"	16		Visited A.D.V.S. office. Two cases evacuated by Mob Amb. One case admitted.	C

WAR DIARY

INTELLIGENCE SUMMARY

Army Form C. 2118.

Place	Date	Hour	Summary of Events and Information	Remarks and references to Appendices
SHEET 27 N29A94	JAN. 17		Visited A.D.V.S. office. Two cases evacuated dil M/S Amb. Sent out F.D.A.C. to collect wounded horses. Three sick cases admitted.	J.S.
"	18		Visited A.D.V.S. office. Eighteen cases evacuated by road to ST. OMER. Sent returns to 23 Div. and flint rollers from 1/5 2/5 & 3/6 4/5 Bdes. Four sick cases admitted.	J.S.
"	19		Visited A.D.V.S. office. Returns rendered. Four sick cases admitted.	J.S.
"	20		Major HIBBARD, A.D.V.S. visited Section. Orders received to prepare for all horses suspected of skin disease in the division. Nineteen cases admitted. Returns rendered.	J.S.
"	21		Returns rendered. Sixty one cases admitted, for suspected skin disease, A.D.V.S. visited Section and inspected the horses. Sent out 1/36 Bty. ONE OR pack from Sub Train.	J.S.
"	22		Sixty even suspected skin cases returned to unit. ONE OR pack from Sub Train.	J.S.

WAR DIARY
INTELLIGENCE SUMMARY
(Erase heading not required.)

Army Form C. 2118.

Instructions regarding War Diaries and Intelligence Summaries are contained in F. S. Regs., Part II. and the Staff Manual respectively. Title Pages will be prepared in manuscript.

[Stamp: MOBILE VETERINARY SECTION No. 12 (London) Date 28/1/17 47th LONDON DIVISION]

Place	Date	Hour	Summary of Events and Information	Remarks and references to Appendices
SHEET 57 JAN. 1.29A.7.4	23		A.D.V.S. visited Section. Horse sent to B.235 By. Fallest mounded horse. Doing pick cases admitted. Visited all companies A.S.C.	
"	24		A.D.V.S. visited Section, also Sanitary Officer who inspected lines and Laterines. Horse sent to D.A.C. Fallest mounded horse. Few sick cases admitted.	
"	25		Thirty six horses evacuated Entrain. Two cases admitted. Visited A.S.C. & F.A. Field Amb.	
"	26		A.D.V.S. visited Section. Horse sent to the 5th Fd. A. R.E. Farlington. Ambro. near cases admitted. Returns rendered.	
"	27		A.D.V.S. visited Section. Officers and other veterinary stores collected from Rutlands for distribution to various units. Visited A.S.C. & Dyers Emb. Returns rendered. Four sick cases admitted.	

Army Form C. 2118.

WAR DIARY
or
INTELLIGENCE SUMMARY
(Erase heading not required.)

Instructions regarding War Diaries and Intelligence Summaries are contained in F. S. Regs., Part II. and the Staff Manual respectively. Title Pages will be prepared in manuscript.

[Stamp: MOBILE VETERINARY SECTION / 47th LONDON DIVISION]

Place	Date	Hour	Summary of Events and Information	Remarks and references to Appendices
SHEET 27 L.29.a.7.4	JAN. 28		Returns received. Principal Commander visited Section and horses. Headquarters A.V.C. attached Section transit horses appearing to Base Hospital HAVRE. Visited 235" Bde. R.F.A. and inspected all horses.	JS
"	29		Two cases evacuated by No.4 Ambulance. T.Co. + men paid. Three cases admitted. Visited all Companies A.S.C. A.D.V.S. visited Section. Two cases evacuated by No.14 Amb. Two cases admitted.	JS
"	30			JS
"	31		Two helpless cases destroyed and buried. One N.Co. + all 10 men attached to Section as working party to collect horses from YPRES. Material for standing brown from R.E. dump. Visited A.S.C. Inspected all horses. Returns rendered.	JS

Southall Capt. A.V.C.

Confidential

Vol 18

WAR DIARY.
of
½ London Mobile Veterinary
Section

From 1. 2. 1914
To 28. 2. 1914

WAR DIARY
INTELLIGENCE SUMMARY
(Erase heading not required.)

Army Form C. 2118.

Place	Date	Hour	Summary of Events and Information	Remarks and references to Appendices
SHEET 21/ L 29 A 7.5	Feb. 1		A.D.V.S. visited Section, also Capt Wilkes. Staff sent to lines of F Batt. Farrier charges. Visited No 1 C. Dog and inspected all horses. Working party sent to YPRES trailer lines. Returns rendered.	J.F.
"	2		Divisional Commander and Staff Officers visited section and inspected horses, also one held A.P.V.S. visited Section. Visited 235 Bde R.F.A. and inspected all horses. One pick was admitted. Returns rendered.	J.F.
"	3		A.P.V.S. visited section. One pick horse admitted. Returns rendered.	J.F.
"	4		Staff went to 141 Bde. M.G.C. Farrier charges. D.A.D.V.S. visited Section and inspected horse standings. Two pick horses admitted. Returns rendered.	J.F.
"	5		A.P.V.S. visited Section. Visited 6 Field Amb. and inspected horses. One sick horse admitted.	J.F.

Kentall Capt. A.V.C.

Army Form C. 2118.

WAR DIARY
INTELLIGENCE SUMMARY
(Erase heading not required.)

Instructions regarding War Diaries and Intelligence Summaries are contained in F. S. Regs., Part II. and the Staff Manual respectively. Title Pages will be prepared in manuscript.

MOBILE VETERINARY SECTION
No. ....
Date .J..2..12
47th LONDON DIVISION

Place	Date	Hour	Summary of Events and Information	Remarks and references to Appendices
SHEET 24. K.29.d.5.	Feb. 6		A.D.V.S. visited Section. Col. MARTIN evacuated sick. Two sick cows admitted.	
"	7		A.D.V.S. visited Section. N.Co. and men paid. Officer Commanding proceeded home on leave.	
"	8		Capt. GOSLING arrived and took over command of this Section. Visited 6 London Field Amb. also No. 1 & 2 Comp. A.S.C. and inspected horses.	
"	9		Major HASTERS visited Section for interview with O.C. Visited No.1 Co. A.S.C. One horse destroyed and buried. Returns rendered.	
"	10		Arrangements received and made for meeting 1X Corps Sup. Coys. waste Section. Sent for bricks etc. One sick cow admitted. Returns rendered.	
"	11		Twelve men from R.F.A. reported to Section to assist in taking 40 horses to 1X Corps Sup. Co. Section detailed to observe lopping for the whole day. Returns rendered. One sick cow admitted.	

2449 Wt. W14957/M90 750,000 1/16 J.B.C. & A. Forms/C.2118/12.

Army Form C. 2118.

WAR DIARY
or
INTELLIGENCE SUMMARY

(Erase heading not required.)

Instructions regarding War Diaries and Intelligence Summaries are contained in F. S. Regs., Part II. and the Staff Manual respectively. Title Pages will be prepared in manuscript.

Place	Date	Hour	Summary of Events and Information	Remarks and references to Appendices
SHEET 24	Feb			
H.Q.47.D.	12		A.D.V.S. visited section. Shoeing party sent to YPRES for shoes. One case admitted.	
"	13		Capt Gosling departed for No. 3 Base Vet. Hospital A.D.V.S. + Capt Pollock visited Section. One sick case admitted.	
"	14		A.D.V.S. visited Section. Indents for veterinary stores received and forwarded. Shoeing party sent to YPRES for shoes	
"	15		Capt McFFIN visited Section to see what progress horses from his Company were making. Pte Britchford retained in hospital.	
"	16		A.D.V.S. visited Section, also AREA COMMANDANT and inspected picket supply and Sanitary Section picket lines. One knee abrasions. Returns rendered.	
"	17		A.D.V.S. visited Section and inspected all horses. One sick case admitted. Returns rendered.	

WAR DIARY or INTELLIGENCE SUMMARY

Army Form C. 2118.

Place	Date	Hour	Summary of Events and Information	Remarks and references to Appendices
SHEET 21. Feb.				
K.21.A.7.5	18		A.S.V.S. visited Section. Pvt. Suggs detained in hospital. Returns rendered. Three sick cases admitted.	
"	19		Two cases evacuated by motor amb. Hosp. sent T.S.&.R. Forwarded. One sick case admitted.	
"	20		Four sickness cases evacuated by motor amb. A.S.V.S. visited Section and ordered distribution of one horse - hired. One sick case admitted.	
"	21		A.S.V.S. visited Section and inspected all horses. Suitable cases were chosen for evacuation on the morrow. Two sick cases admitted.	
"	22		Twenty two cases evacuated by Road. A.S.V.S. visited Section. Surrock case admitted.	
"	23		A.S.V.S. visited Section. Pvt. Boren arrived from base. Four sick cases admitted. Returns rendered.	

Army Form C. 2118.

WAR DIARY
INTELLIGENCE SUMMARY
(Erase heading not required.)

Place	Date	Hour	Summary of Events and Information	Remarks and references to Appendices
SHEET 27 K29a7.5	Feb. 24		Lime for all units 47th Division drawn from Corps dip. Material to-day standing drawn from R.E. Pack huggs exchanged from hospital. Two sick men admitted. Returns rendered.	S.
"	25		Officer Commanding returned from leave. A.D.V.S. visited Section. Visited No 2 C.A.D.S. at night, in answer to urgent call. Four sick men admitted. Returns rendered.	S.
"	26		A.D.V.S. visited Section. Visited No 2 C. A.S.C. from the urgent case, horse much better. Labour parties returned to Batts. N.Co + men paid. Six sick men admitted.	S.
"	27		Visited two slaughter trains arrangements for disposal of carcases fit for human consumption. A.D.V.S. visited Section. Two sick men admitted.	S.
"	28		Horse sold to slaughterman. A.D.V.S. visited Section. Four sick men admitted. Returns rendered.	S.

Ronald Cope A.V.C. T

Confidential. No. 19

WAR DIARY
of
½ London Mobile Veterinary Section

From 1.3.17
To 31.3.17

Army Form C. 2118.

WAR DIARY
or
INTELLIGENCE SUMMARY
(Erase heading not required.)

Instructions regarding War Diaries and Intelligence Summaries are contained in F. S. Regs., Part II. and the Staff Manual respectively. Title Pages will be prepared in manuscript.

Place	Date	Hour	Summary of Events and Information	Remarks and references to Appendices
SHEET 21 L.29.a.7.4	MARCH 1		A.D.V.S. visited Section. Shifty six horses evacuated but and Three horses destroyed and buried. Two sick cases admitted. Returns rendered.	J.S.
"	2		Visited and inspected horses of 235 Bde R.F.A. One other rank admitted to hospital. Returns rendered.	J.S.
"	3		A.D.V.S. visited Section. Also Capt Whippin to see when his horses would be fit for work. Two letters from IX Corps Sup. for use of division. Sire sick cases admitted. Returns rendered.	J.S.
"	4		A.D.A.M.G. visited Section and inspected stores. Visited Mob. Sect. D.A.C. and inspected all horses. D.D.V.S. visited Section. One other rank rejoined Section.	J.S.
"	5		A.D.V.S. visited Section. Visited and inspected horses of 235 Bde R.F.A. Two other ranks inoculated	J.S.

Army Form C. 2118.

WAR DIARY
INTELLIGENCE SUMMARY
(Erase heading not required.)

Place	Date	Hour	Summary of Events and Information	Remarks and references to Appendices
SHEET 27 L29d.7.4	March 6		Four sick cases admitted. ONE horse sick and ONE destroyed. Greaves returned and buried.	
"	7		Two sick cases admitted. Visited and inspected No.4 Sect. I.A.C. also H.Q. and Signal Co. horses.	
"	8		Having visited section with Corps Commandant and inspected sick horses and sheds. Seventeen sick cases evacuated by road. A.D.V.S. visited Section. One sick cases admitted. Clipped machine returned to section.	
"	9		Visited and inspected horses of Signal Co. and H.Q. A.D.V.S. visited Section. Returns rendered.	
"	10		Two sick cases admitted. Visited No.4 Sect. I.A.C. and inspected horses. Form filled from F.Corps H.Q. Returns rendered.	

Army Form C. 2118.

WAR DIARY
INTELLIGENCE SUMMARY
(Erase heading not required.)

Instructions regarding War Diaries and Intelligence Summaries are contained in F.S. Regs., Part II. and the Staff Manual respectively. Title Pages will be prepared in manuscript.

Place	Date	Hour	Summary of Events and Information	Remarks and references to Appendices
SHEET 29 K29d.7.4	March 11		Hart sent to C236 Bty to collect lame horse. Corp RELF returned station from 140 Inf Bde. Visited No.4 Sect. D.A.C. A.D.V.S. visited section. Four sick horses admitted. Returns rendered.	
"	12		Visited Field Cookers, also H.Q. and Signal Co. and inspected horses. Four sick cases admitted. N.Co. men paid.	
"	13		One horse destroyed, knacker sold for 175fr. Two R.A.M.C. officers visited station and examined one other rank who was ordered to hospital. Four sick cases admitted.	
"	14		A.D.V.S. visited section. Hart sent to B236 Bty to collect lame horse. Visited and inspected horses of A236 Bty. Three sick cases admitted.	
"	15		Twenty two sick cases evacuated Dulnoon. A.D.V.S. visited section, also Capt. BAWDIN reported for duty. One other rank left by horse detained in hospital. Hart sent to T.M Bath. to collect horse. Three sick cases admitted.	

Army Form C. 2118.

WAR DIARY
INTELLIGENCE SUMMARY
(Erase heading not required.)

Instructions regarding War Diaries and Intelligence Summaries are contained in F. S. Regs., Part II. and the Staff Manual respectively. Title Pages will be prepared in manuscript.

Place	Date	Hour	Summary of Events and Information	Remarks and references to Appendices
SHEET 24. March K29d 7.4	16		One horse destroyed and carcase sold for 175 fr. Two sick cases admitted. Visited H.R. Signal Co. and inspected horses. Two sick cases admitted. Returns rendered.	J.
"	17		A.D.V.S. visited section. also D.A.A.Q.M.G. & Capt. HOUSE who inspected sick horses and standings. One horse destroyed and carcase sold for 175 fr. Two sick cases admitted. Returns rendered.	J.
"	18		A.D.V.S. visited section. Visited H.Q. and Signal Co. and inspected horses. Returns rendered.	J.
"	19		Two sick cases admitted. Two other horses inoculated. A.D.V.S. visited section.	J.
"	20		Officers from 6 L.J. Amb. & ⅙ R.W.F. visited section to inspect and collect temperaments. Eleven sick cases admitted, also one stray mule.	J.
"	21		Sixteen horses cast by D.D.V.R. for reasons of destruction admitted. Also received that one other horse had the horse on 15th evacuated to England. Four sick cases admitted. A.D.V.S. visited section.	J.

Army Form C. 2118.

WAR DIARY
of
INTELLIGENCE SUMMARY
(Erase heading not required.)

Instructions regarding War Diaries and Intelligence Summaries are contained in F. S. Regs., Part II. and the Staff Manual respectively. Title Pages will be prepared in manuscript.

MOBILE VETERINARY SECTION
No. 1/2 London
Date 22.3.17
47th LONDON DIVISION

Place	Date	Hour	Summary of Events and Information	Remarks and references to Appendices
SHEET 27 L2&6.7.4	March 22		Unit sent to Halifax Camp to collect charges. Twelve sick cases admitted and evacuated by road. Remounts received by A.D.V.S.	
"	23		A.D.V.S. visited section also Capt Guig. Two sick cases admitted. Returns rendered.	
"	24		Two cases taken for inspection by D.D.V.R. A.D.V.S. visited section. Visited H.Q. and Signal Co. and inspected horses. Returns rendered.	
"	25		Returns rendered. Two sick cases admitted.	
"	26		Unit sent to 17 C.o.L. Kettle mounted force. Two oblit. hands circulated. Four sick cases admitted. A.D.V.S. visited section.	
"	27		Eighteen horses cast by D.D.V.R. taken to Field Remount Section. A.A.Q.M.G. and A.D.V.S. visited section. Unit sent to D.A.C. to collect lame mule. One horse died. Horses skinned & buried. Seventeen sick cases admitted.	

WAR DIARY
INTELLIGENCE SUMMARY
(Erase heading not required.)

Army Form C. 2118.

Place	Date	Hour	Summary of Events and Information	Remarks and references to Appendices
SHEET 27 L29d 7.4.	MARCH 28		A.D.V.S. visited Section. Four sick cases admitted. Second rate sent to slaughter house and slaughter of horses sent by D.D.R. unable to accept for over a week.	J.S.
"	29		Thirty seven cases evacuated by rail, including horses sent for destruction. Sent to D.A.C. Collecting Stn. mule. Inspected horses of Signal Co. One other sent detained in hospital with trench fever.	J.S.
"	30		A.V.S. visited Section and arranged for his horses and grooms to be attached. One sick case admitted. Returns rendered.	J.S.
"	31		D.A.A.R.M.G. visited Section and inspected also ones standings. A.D.V.S. visited Section. Returns rendered.	J.S.

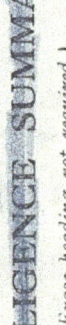

Lowshaw
Capt. A.V.C.

Confidential

Vol 20

WAR DIARY

of

½ London Mobile Veterinary Section
47th London Div.

From 1.4.17
To 30.4.17

Army Form C. 2118.

WAR DIARY
INTELLIGENCE SUMMARY
(Erase heading not required.)

Instructions regarding War Diaries and Intelligence Summaries are contained in F. S. Regs., Part II. and the Staff Manual respectively. Title pages will be prepared in manuscript.

Place	Date	Hour	Summary of Events and Information	Remarks and references to Appendices
SHEET 27. L 29 & 35	APRIL 1		D.A.Q.M.G. visited section with Capt Pollock and inspected horses and stores. Two horses destroyed and buried. Two sick cases admitted. One sick case admitted. Returns rendered.	
"	2		Camp Commandant with D.A.Q.M.G. visited section and inspected stables. One mount received from R.A.F. Six sick cases admitted.	
"	3		Special train load of sick horses issued and despatched. Three men in charge of train. Two horses destroyed at station and buried. 28½ mouths sick. One horse sent to Corps Q.S. Twelve sick cases admitted.	
"	4		A.D.V.S. visited section. Six sick cases admitted.	
"	5		Twenty two sick cases evacuated by train. Three sick cases admitted. A.D.V.S. visited station to sign forms in absence of A.C.	

WAR DIARY

INTELLIGENCE SUMMARY.

(Erase heading not required.)

Army Form C. 2118.

Place	Date	Hour	Summary of Events and Information	Remarks and references to Appendices
SHEET 34 APRIL				
L 29.A.7.3	6		O.C. returned from Base Vet Hospital (No.3). Visited H.Q and Signal Co. and inspected horses, also 3 Mr Labouille attrass A.D.V.S. Conference in afternoon. Five sick cases admitted. Returns rendered.	JB
"	7		A.D.V.S. visited Section. Thirteen sick cases admitted. Returns rendered.	JB
"	8		Returns rendered. Twelve sick cases from attached Bde R.F.A. admitted A.D.V.S. visited Section.	JB
"	9		Camp Commandant visited station and inspected sheep shears & emerge. Five sick cases admitted. Inspected horses of H.Q. and signal Co.	JB
"	10		Visited Veterinary Station D.A.C. and inspected all horses. L.D.S. worked section. Eleven sick cases admitted.	JB
"	11		A.D.V.S. visited Station. Four sick cases admitted.	JB

WAR DIARY
INTELLIGENCE SUMMARY.
(Erase heading not required.)

Army Form C. 2118.

Instructions regarding War Diaries and Intelligence Summaries are contained in F. S. Regs., Part II. and the Staff Manual respectively. Title pages will be prepared in manuscript.

Place	Date	Hour	Summary of Events and Information	Remarks and references to Appendices
SHEET 21	APRIL			
29.d.7.6.	12		Forty two sick horses evacuated. Lifted, buried cow & one sick, cleaned and buried	
			Divisional Commander visited section and inspected horse ambulance.	
			One sick case admitted. Names of N.C.O.s shown for A/Cpl & A/L/Cpl submitted.	
			One L/Cpl returned to duty from Rest Camp.	
"	13		A.D.V.S. visited station. Visited H.Q. and Signal Co. also 2nd Div. Tunnel Batt.	
			and inspected horse standard ordinary. Returns rendered.	
"	14		A.D. in charge of VIII Corps Horse Lib. Evac'd but horse sent for'd Station)	
			Also sick case admitted. Returns rendered.	
"	15		A.D.V.S. visited station. One sick case admitted. Returns rendered.	
"	16		Brick and sand collected from railhead for rebuilding standings	
			One L/Cpl sent to duty to duty from X Cav Lib. A.V. on discharge	

WAR DIARY

INTELLIGENCE SUMMARY

Army Form C. 2118.

Place	Date	Hour	Summary of Events and Information	Remarks and references to Appendices
SHEET 24	APRIL			
L.M.O.D.S.	17		Got sick cases in section and sick horses sent to VIII Corps Sick Horse area. Cases evacuated by Artl Ambulance. Personnel composed mostly of section and inspected all horses and also occurred in horses that have been to the air not having been gassed. The inoculation was finished. 2nd sick cases admitted	
"	18		In relation horses sick. F.M.R.L.S., endid Colombier 53 No dismounted Horse Stores and linned. Visited H.Q. and Signal Co. and inspected all horses. No M.Co. from Sick Unit, visited section and inspected sick horses. Any sick case admitted	
"	19		0975 visited sections, one horse sick observed twice. Imports case admitted	
"	20		Visited R.O.C. H.Q. Signal Co. and inspected horses. Attend and Conference. Three sick cases admitted. Returns rendered.	
"	21		2 Mules horses sent to VIII Corps Sick Returns rendered	

Army Form C. 2118.

WAR DIARY
INTELLIGENCE SUMMARY.
(Erase heading not required.)

Instructions regarding War Diaries and Intelligence Summaries are contained in F. S. Regs., Part II. and the Staff Manual respectively. Title pages will be prepared in manuscript.

[Stamp: MOBILE VETERINARY SECTION No. 2 Date 22.4.17 47th LONDON DIVISION]

Place	Date	Hour	Summary of Events and Information	Remarks and references to Appendices
SHEET 27 1.29.d.7.6.	APRIL 22		O.i/c visited station and inspected the lines and THREE private billets for duty to X Corps lkly. Attachment. Equipment and stores sent for necessary work. J.D.V.S. 2 Army Called.	
"	23		O.i/c visited station, also A.P.M. Traffic Officer, D.D.O.S., D.A.Q.M.G., Dept went. Capt. Gillies N.C.O. and men paid. Two sick horses admitted. Violet spirit. D.A.C.	
"	24		Now new attached X Corps said. 16 and sent 6 X Corps AAC. Two sick horses admitted.	
"	25		Visited H.Q. and Signal Co. and inspected horses. Severely injured horse admitted from attached Bde. R.F.A. Slight attention supplied to attend sick horses.	
"	26		Duty sick horse evacuated by road. Two sick horses admitted. Visited A Station D.A.C. and inspected horses.	
"	27		Visited H.Q. Sig. Co. reinspected horses. One sick horse admitted. Attended Conference. Chief Vet.	

Army Form C. 2118.

WAR DIARY

INTELLIGENCE SUMMARY.

(Erase heading not required.)

Place	Date	Hour	Summary of Events and Information	Remarks and references to Appendices
SHEET 24 APRIL				
L.29.a.7.5.	28		Capt Eng went to station, took over D.A.C. inspected horses. 2 minor cases.	JB
"	29		Visits H.Q and dept to get supplies at horse. Eye cattle run returned from areas of strong [?] being again Hotel. Two pack were sent to return nearest.	JB
"	30		Visits Det lecture D.A.C inspected horses. 8 pack mules sick in marked [?]. Returned. received Attached now returned to Base.	JB

[signature] Capt A/C

Confidential Vol 21

WAR DIARY

of

1/2 korean Mobile Veterinary Section

From 1.5.17 To/ 31.5.17

WAR DIARY or INTELLIGENCE SUMMARY

Army Form C. 2118.

Place	Date	Hour	Summary of Events and Information	Remarks and references to Appendices
SHEET 24 L 29.A.7.4	MAY 1		O.R.T.S. awaited Section. Returns received. Sent skin taken unmounted. Visited H.Q Signal Co. and inspected horses.	
"	2		Twenty two sick horses admitted. Two horses received. One sheet received during the night. Hot mixtures applied. Tube at 4th short.	
"	3		Down to four sick horses evacuated buttons. Winter clothing sent to O.Stores received. Horses sent to 15 Batt failed have been visited. H.Q and Signal Co horses. Camp Commandant visited stables. Two sick horses admitted.	
"	4		O.R.T.S. awaited Section. Also train troops. One Officer's horse shot lame. Horse sent to Dock here from B.235 Bty Horses O.R.T.S inspected. Four sick horses admitted. Returns rendered.	
"	5		Returns rendered. Visited H.Q. Signal Co + Sig Coy. H.Q. and inspected horses. Two sick horses admitted.	

WAR DIARY
or
INTELLIGENCE SUMMARY.

Army Form C. 2118.

Place	Date	Hour	Summary of Events and Information	Remarks and references to Appendices
SHEET 27				
L29 a 7.4	6		Two serjent cases evacuated by Mob Ambulance. C.R.S. Visited Section. One sick case admitted. Returns rendered.	
"	7		Goat sent to collect horse from II 236 Bty, shot wounds. Shoe been secured, visited A.D.V.S. Du duty and wounded horses. Two cases admitted.	
"	8		Two sick cases admitted. Visited sent to X Corps Slip. Goat collected wounded horse from R.W.F. Evacuation still carried on from I.D.R. Visited H.Q. Signal Co and collected horse. C.R.S. visited Section.	
"	9		Eight sick cases admitted. One collected by Goat from R.W.F. Line horse secured. Visited H.Q. Signal Co horse Lines.	
"	10		Seventy four cases evacuated to field; two hybrids Ambulance, that one to collect wounded horse from 515 R.E. Veterinary officers shot and bullet secured. C.R.S. visited Section.	

Army Form C. 2118.

WAR DIARY
or
INTELLIGENCE SUMMARY.
(Erase heading not required.)

Instructions regarding War Diaries and Intelligence Summaries are contained in F. S. Regs., Part II. and the Staff Manual respectively. Title pages will be prepared in manuscript.

Place	Date	Hour	Summary of Events and Information	Remarks and references to Appendices
SHEET 27 L.29.d.7.4	11		Returning O.R.S. mobile Section. One man reports Sickness. Lot a case of horse shivering. Attend O.R.S. Section. Two sick cases admitted.	
"	12		D.D.V.S. visited Section and inspected horses and linings. Two sick cases admitted. Sick horses sent through 3rd Tunbury Composition. Visited M.R and Sigd Co. provided C two remain.	
"	13		P.M. sick on horse that sent pertonito O.R.S. also D.D.V. visited Section. New Stabl sheds inoculated one sick case admitted.	
"	14		One Stableman sent to sick at + Corps Horse Disp recommitted to hospital unfit for our admitted. Visited HQ Signl Co 4th DD Coy and inspected horses.	
"	15		O.D.V.S. visited Mobile Section. One sick case admitted.	

WAR DIARY
or
INTELLIGENCE SUMMARY.

(Erase heading not required.)

Army Form C. 2118.

Place	Date	Hour	Summary of Events and Information	Remarks and references to Appendices
SHEET 27 A.29.C.7.4.	16		Lieut Park again examined the 135th Battalion. One like served	
			A&S. Mobile Section. One officer attended Sick Lines and discharged	
			two horses. Visited M.D. Sick Lines and inspected horses this Bde. evacuated	
	17		A.V.3. and A.D.V.S. Mobile Section went out to 0236c.9.4. to e0236c.9.7. to witness A-wards.	
			Lieut Parr and Eacheson from B236c.8.4. Horses duly inspected.	
	18		Went into hospital. Officer of Sir Bernard Walsh N.O. in response	
			to Agent Wm attended A.V.S. interview. Returned sentence.	
	19		Capt Brimdon went to visit duties early informing Lieut Parr to his	
			Command the Sib Gr. visited stables and evening how two horses to the	
			inspected. Also saw horses and horse holders inspecting various	
			examined by A&S inluence. Returned senior.	

Army Form C. 2118.

WAR DIARY
or
INTELLIGENCE SUMMARY.
(Erase heading not required.)

Instructions regarding War Diaries and Intelligence Summaries are contained in F.S. Regs., Part II. and the Staff Manual respectively. Title pages will be prepared in manuscript.

Place	Date	Hour	Summary of Events and Information	Remarks and references to Appendices
SHEET 27				
L.29a7.4.	20		ADVS visited section. One other rank returned from X Corps Horse Std. He having been examined. Return rendered.	
"	21		ADVS visited sections. Also for purposes from BAC Park, Butchford procured on loan. Sent forth for horse sent held Mostemparl	
"	22		ADVS proceeded on leave C.the Letry appointed A/ADVS Divisional Command visited section to see the plough and observed extraction with care and attention given. Sent sent forth of wounded horse from D.A.C. Visited H.Q. Signal Co. & D. In Coty. and inspected horses. One case admitted.	
"	23		Visited ADVS office. Visited and inspected transport of F Batt. One horse received. No sick cases admitted.	
"	24		Visited ADVS office. Inspected horse of HQ Signal Co. no sick case admitted	

A1945. Wt. W11422/M1160 350,000 12/16 D.D.&L. Forms/C/2118/14.

WAR DIARY
or
INTELLIGENCE SUMMARY.
(Erase heading not required.)

Army Form C. 2118.

Place	Date	Hour	Summary of Events and Information	Remarks and references to Appendices
SHEET 27 L.29.d.7.4.	25		Returns finished. Visited ADVS. Afternoon writing and phoning up meeting of POS in afternoon. Visited H.Q. 53rd Bde. and inspected horses. One sick case admitted.	
	26		Request for interview by Divisional Commander complied with. Visited ADVS. Office. One horse cast for (507). Carcase removed from M.D.S. C.O. opened and burned. One sick case. Returns rendered. Thunderstorm broke over the morning.	
SHEET 27 G.34.B.8.10	27		Station moved to G.34.B.8.10. after having waited at L. Raba 20 Junge to 6 horsed field Art. wagon Obs. Sick case left behind in charge of one man. One sick case admitted.	
"	28		Inspected horses of MC Inf. Bde. Went out to their horse form 83 Jum 20 Corps Commercial (?) ADVS visited section and inspected demonstration. Sanitary filled with section. One sick case admitted.	

Army Form C. 2118.

WAR DIARY
or
INTELLIGENCE SUMMARY.
(Erase heading not required.)

Instructions regarding War Diaries and Intelligence Summaries are contained in F. S. Regs., Part II. and the Staff Manual respectively. Title pages will be prepared in manuscript.

Place	Date	Hour	Summary of Events and Information	Remarks and references to Appendices
SHEET 28				
G34.6.8.10	29		Sent out to 20 Battn and B104.B17 to collect wounded horses. Visited A&7S Office also H.Q. Signal Co. no wounded horses English pier evacuated.	
"	30		Visited A&7S Officer, also visited A&7S 44 Dist, sent out supply pack horses sent out to collect wounded horses from Dug Out. three horses received him sick ones admitted	
"	31		Thirty three cases evacuated. Sent out to collect horses from #D.A.C. Seven three cases admitted. Visited A&7S officer. Return journey.	

Confidential.

WAR DIARY

of

½ London Mobile Veterinary Section

From 1.6.17 to 30.6.17

Vol 22

WAR DIARY
INTELLIGENCE SUMMARY

(Erase heading not required.)

Place	Date	Hour	Summary of Events and Information	Remarks and references to Appendices
SHEET 28	JUNE			
A.34.b.5.10	1		Visited A.D.V.S. office in morning and present our conference of Vety officers in afternoon. Returns rendered	
"	2		Visited A.D.V.S. office. Shotgun pieces horse admitted and one destroyed. One sick mule returned to duty from X Cavy M.I.D. Two horses received. Returns rendered	
"	3		Visited A.D.V.S. office. Capt. Colling R.V.C. reports at section on return from leave. Went out to 111 H.B. treated wounded horse. Dubrovice's mare admitted. Returns. Survey. Compositions, no manoeuvre as possible winter to enfly	
"	4		Camp pitched in morning. horses taken to safety. Visited C.R.H. on return from leave. Sur. attel unto Hosmer fainb. heavy innibeani. by cause of okasioning. Went out to pitch line from 110 B6 A.F.A. One sick horse admitted	
"	5		Lieutenant Comanding A.A.V.M.C. visited section and inspected horses and shoes. One pint to 14 Bge R.H.A. treated wounded horse. Sent by him sent to X Cavy S.L.O.	

Army Form C. 2118.

WAR DIARY
INTELLIGENCE SUMMARY

(Erase heading not required.)

Army Form C. 2118.

Place	Date	Hour	Summary of Events and Information	Remarks and references to Appendices
SHEET 25	JUNE			
G.34.b.9.10.	6		Went out to 141Bde A.F.A. Installed horse S.F. sick cases admitted. One Corp. and two men sent on advanced dressing post at PIONEER CAMP. Two stations furnished in Corps. Fourteen sick cases admitted. R.&D. men sick.	
"	7		One still mules returned to duty with X Corps M.V.S. Went out to #7 D.A.C. trotting horse. Two sick cases admitted. One horse sick. Tetanus — one case buried.	
"	8		Seventy-five sick cases evacuated by road. Three Hort. cases evacuated by rail. Ambulance. Two sick cases admitted. Attended V.O. enquiries. Stamp. Received.	
"	9		O.R.S. writes section. Stat. out to bt 8th Forfar. mounted Bde to 4 Bde. R.M.O. Are sick cases admitted. Stamp verified.	
"	10		Veterinary Staff received. Return sending O.R.S. mobile section. Spec. sick cases admitted.	

Army Form C. 2118.

Instructions regarding War Diaries and Intelligence Summaries are contained in F. S. Regs., Part II. and the Staff Manual respectively. Title pages will be prepared in manuscript.

WAR DIARY
INTELLIGENCE SUMMARY.
(Erase heading not required.)

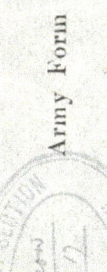

Place	Date	Hour	Summary of Events and Information	Remarks and references to Appendices
SHEET 28	JUNE			
G.34.6.6.10	11.		Shot cart two sick horses from 109H.Bty. k16 sick acting for return of men from X Corps M.V.S. as per instructions from D.D.V.S. A.G.V.S. mobile section	
"	12		Shot sent to 109 Bde also #7 Div signal Co two sick horses. Received twenty sick horses tomorrow. Two others received in morning, one other sick horse in eve. Seven sick cases admitted.	
"	13		Twenty sick horses evacuated to X Corps Collecting Station. Section moved to G.32.d.5.1. Thirty sick cases admitted from 76 Bde A.F.A.	
G.32.d.8.1.	14		Fifty sick horses evacuated to X Corps C.S. by special permission of D.D.V.S. also A.G.V.S. 30 Div. mobile section. Ten sick cases admitted.	
"	15		Party sent to line opened over two teams A.G.V.S. mobile section and kits examined at H.Q. Shot sent to #7 Div H.Q. to collect horse. Thirteen sick cases admitted. Returns received Corp R/s Lts etc & Settlers; S.S. Lewis & S.S. Corps.	

WAR DIARY
INTELLIGENCE SUMMARY.
(Erase heading not required.)

Army Form C. 2118.

Instructions regarding War Diaries and Intelligence Summaries are contained in F. S. Regs., Part II. and the Staff Manual respectively. Title pages will be prepared in manuscript.

Place	Date	Hour	Summary of Events and Information	Remarks and references to Appendices
SHEET 28 G.30.d.7.1.	JUNE 16		R.A.S moved with H.Q. to BEARING HEAD. One mule attacked by horse, destroyed & buried, one buried. Returns rendered.	
"	17		Capt Alexander visited Section and inspected horse lines & standings. One horse sick, starved and buried. Rifles and ammo issued to X Corps C.S.	
"	18		Capt Lumb visited Section. NCO's riders paid.	
"	19		Horse sent to IX Corps M.V.S. buried of D.D.V.S. buried – one sick admitted. Horse and inspected horses & Riders & by request. O.C. 52 M.V.S. visited Section.	
"	20		Instruction to effect issue of 10H.B.A.B. DeathI send returned from leave, one sick adm. Returns rendered by D.R.S. due on 21 inst.	
"	21		R.A.S visits Section and held conference of P.Os. Two sick horses admitted from sick lines transferred. Sice sick cases admitted. Returns rendered.	

WAR DIARY
INTELLIGENCE SUMMARY
(Erase heading not required.)

Army Form C. 2118.

Instructions regarding War Diaries and Intelligence Summaries are contained in F. S. Regs., Part II. and the Staff Manual respectively. Title pages will be prepared in manuscript.

Place	Date	Hour	Summary of Events and Information	Remarks and references to Appendices
SHEET 26	JUNE			
G32 d & 1.	22		Sent out to collect wounded horse from B236B4. Two horses sick, above, and lived at Gypp's forward on base. Thirteen sick cases admitted. Returns received.	
"	23		Pole Mackler arrived at Sutton forestry troubles are dept transferred. One sick case admitted. Returns received.	
"	24		Sent R.E.t proceed to 50 M.Y.S for duty. Two cases evacuated by flat Fx.Corps C.S.	
"	25		One sick horse evacuated by Mot Ambulance, one evacuated by flat to X Corps M.V.H. also killed. One man detailed to interring party. Two sick cases admitted.	
"	26		S.S. Corps attached reported for duty to replace S.S. Cpl. ——— and transferred. Seven sick cases admitted.	
"	27		Notice received to have an N.Co. transport to inspect our horse stock sent to collect horse from 92 Cph. Two sick cases admitted.	

Army Form C. 2118.

WAR DIARY
INTELLIGENCE SUMMARY.
(Erase heading not required.)

Instructions regarding War Diaries and Intelligence Summaries are contained in F. S. Regs., Part II. and the Staff Manual respectively. Title pages will be prepared in manuscript.

Place	Date	Hour	Summary of Events and Information	Remarks and references to Appendices
SHEET 28 G 32 A.8.L.	JUNE 28		S.S. Corp Lewis proceeded to No. 24 FA Field Hospital. Cpl. S. posted Lewis and held a carriers of T.O. No one now admitted. Return renewed.	
"	29		Cpl. S. T/Sgt. Smith moved section and inspected etc. also relearning. T.O. provides new site and found the section occupying was not moving out on the matter. New lines enrolled by 17.00. Return renewed.	
"	30		Return rendered. One case admitted. One horse destroyed — flayed and buried. One man sent to take over from 52 M.V.S. Packed ready to move in morning	

[signature] Capt AVC

A6945 Wt. W11422/M1160 350,000 12/16 D. D. & L. Forms/C/2118/14.

Confidential Vol 23

WAR DIARY
of
1/2 London Mobile Veterinary Section.
47th(London) Div.

From 1.7.17
To 31.7.17

Army Form C. 2118.

WAR DIARY
INTELLIGENCE SUMMARY.
(Erase heading not required.)

Instructions regarding War Diaries and Intelligence Summaries are contained in F. S. Regs., Part II, and the Staff Manual respectively. Title pages will be prepared in manuscript.

Place	Date	Hour	Summary of Events and Information	Remarks and references to Appendices
SHEET 28 N.7.a.5.5	July 1		Section moved to N.7.a.5.5 taking out and from 32 M.V.S. Eleven sick cases left and taken out by this Section. Returns rendered.	
"	2		H.Q.V.S. visited Section and inspected shoes, stampings and billets. Fourteen sick cases admitted.	
"	3		H.Q.V.S. visited Section. Arrangements made for inspection of Exhibitors horses from all units in the division on the morrow. Six sick cases admitted.	
"	4		H.Q.V.S. and all V.Os. Division visited Section. Ninety six post horses inspected and particulars of each taken. Ten cases admitted. Nco and men present.	
"	5		Horse sent to H.Q. 190 Bde. trecklar horse wounded. Fifteen sick cases admitted.	
"	6		Fifty two sick cases evacuated by road. Twelve sick cases admitted. Horse sent to B 190 Bde. to collect wounded horses. Returns rendered.	

Army Form C. 2118.

WAR DIARY
INTELLIGENCE SUMMARY.
(Erase heading not required.)

Instructions regarding War Diaries and Intelligence Summaries are contained in F. S. Regs., Part II. and the Staff Manual respectively. Title pages will be prepared in manuscript.

Place	Date	Hour	Summary of Events and Information	Remarks and references to Appendices
SHEET 28. JULY				
N.7.a.5.5.	7		Four wounded horses rec'd, exined, reserve dunies. Float sent to collect injured horse from 2/3 Cav. Reg. Twenty four sick horses evac'd admitted. D.A.D.V.S. visited section. Returns rendered.	
"	8		D.A.D.V.S. Capts. Bryan & Edwards visited section and her horse on Pvt. TILBURY who qualified for Shoeingsmith. Returns rendered.	
"	9		One horse sick and one destroyed. Both exined and reserve duties. Sire sick horses admitted. Shaft of float broken.	
"	10		Float sent to X Corps workshop for repair. Visited 124 H.Bty. Two wounded horses. One horse destroyed, exined, reserve duties. Six sick horses admitted.	
"	11		D.A.D.V.S. visited section. Also V.O. Division and inspected one hundred post horses. Four "T.V." men reported for duties for light duty from 51 Field Amb. Seven sick horses admitted.	

WAR DIARY

INTELLIGENCE SUMMARY.

Army Form C. 2118.

Place	Date	Hour	Summary of Events and Information	Remarks and references to Appendices
SHEET 2	JULY			
N.7.A.V.S.	12		Sergt HILL-WALDEN reported as detach for duty. to replace two sergts proceeded on transferred. Two horses destroyed, skinned + carcass buried. Fifteen sick cases admitted. Visited X Corps workshop re repair of float.	
"	13		Float collected from X Corps workshop. One N.C.O + five men borrowed from 104 Bde to assist in evacuation of eighty seven sick horses. Six sick cases admitted. Return rendered.	
"	14		Two sick horses and twelve hides evacuated by Motor Ambulance. Two sick cases admitted. Return rendered. Sergt Walden posted to X Corps M.V.S.	
"	15		Motor Ambulance collar trailer. Two wounded horses and twelve hides. Two sick cases admitted. Return rendered. Visited horse slaughtered re disposal of twenty horses	
"	16		Two wounded horses + hides evacuated by Motor Amb. Horse taken for slaughter and sold for 75 fr. N Co. men paid. Five sick cases admitted.	

Army Form C. 2118.

WAR DIARY
INTELLIGENCE SUMMARY.
(Erase heading not required.)

Instructions regarding War Diaries and Intelligence Summaries are contained in F. S. Regs., Part II. and the Staff Manual respectively. Title pages will be prepared in manuscript.

Place	Date	Hour	Summary of Events and Information	Remarks and references to Appendices
SHEET 28	July			
M.V.S.	17		One horse destroyed, skinned & carcass buried. One horse cob for slaughter for 175ft. Thirty pc sick horses received from Australian F.A.B. Sixteen sick cases admitted.	
"	18		One Offr. Supt. received letter from I Corps M.V.S. The transfer to 22 M.V.S. Eighteen sick cases admitted. Inspected debility horses in charge of D.A.D.V.S.	
"	19		Heat went to collect wounded horses from III Aust. F.A.B. One horse cob for slaughter for 175ft. Eleven sick cases admitted.	
"	20		Hot Ambulance called for one horse and forty hides. Thirty pc sick horses evacuated by road. One horse cob for slaughter for 175ft. Ten sick cases admitted. Returns handed.	
"	21		A.D.V.S. I Corps paid station inspected. horses suffering from skin disease. One mule cob for slaughter for 150ft. Eleven sick cases admitted. Returns handed.	

Army Form C. 2118.

WAR DIARY
INTELLIGENCE SUMMARY.
(Erase heading not required.)

Instructions regarding War Diaries and Intelligence Summaries are contained in F. S. Regs., Part II. and the Staff Manual respectively. Title pages will be prepared in manuscript.

Place	Date	Hour	Summary of Events and Information	Remarks and references to Appendices
SHEET 28	JULY			
M.7 a 8.5	22		One horse ordered for slaughter for 135H. Twelve sick cases admitted. Braves reward to now on the matter.	
G 32.A.9.0	23		Section moved to G 32.a.9.0. Eight horses handed out to 41 D.I.M.V.S. Twenty four sick cases taken. Whole section has to now dismounted as all the riding horses have been by the conducting party when evacuating. One sick case admitted.	
"	24		Stables and sheds limewashed, standings disinfected. Two cases admitted.	
"	25		D.A.D.V.S. with V.O. division inspected debilitated horses. One sick case evacuated on leave. These still have to surrender it to section. One sick case admitted.	
"	26		D.A.D.V.S. proceeded over N.O. division in conference. Staff Sergt reported to 22 M.V.S. for duty. Two sick cases admitted.	
"	27		Twenty four sick cases evacuated. A.D.V.S. + D.A.D.V.S. visited section. One sick case admitted.	

Army Form C. 2118.

WAR DIARY
INTELLIGENCE SUMMARY.
(Erase heading not required.)

Instructions regarding War Diaries and Intelligence Summaries are contained in F. S. Regs., Part II. and the Staff Manual respectively. Title pages will be prepared in manuscript.

Place	Date	Hour	Summary of Events and Information	Remarks and references to Appendices
G.32.A.9.O.	July 28		Two pick cases evacuated by train, one man sent on conducting party. D.A.D.V.S. visited section. Stray animals collected by H.Q. Div. Arty. Returns rendered.	
"	29		One permanent mobile section re authn of unspected. One pick case admitted. Visits to suppurat and inspected horses of Canadian Field Co. R.E. Returns rendered.	
"	30		Capt Burton visited section. Inspected horses from 4th & 5th Field Art. the two proposed to start units. Two pick cases admitted. NCOs men paid.	
"	31		D.A.D.V.S. with A.P.M. visited section. Took pick to H.Q. H.O. Inf. Bde. Feeller horse Capt Curtis visited section. Two horses admitted no progressing. Returns rendered.	

[signature]

Confidential. No 24

WAR DIARY

of

½ London Mobile Veterinary Section
47th London Dn.

From 1.5.17 To 31.5.17

Army Form C. 2118.

WAR DIARY
INTELLIGENCE SUMMARY.
(Erase heading not required.)

Instructions regarding War Diaries and Intelligence Summaries are contained in F. S. Regs., Part II. and the Staff Manual respectively. Title pages will be prepared in manuscript.

Place	Date	Hour	Summary of Events and Information	Remarks and references to Appendices
SHEET 2T	August			
G 32 a 9.0	1		A.D.V.S. visited Section and inspected all debilitated horses of the Division. Remotalls from remounts returned to Section. One sick case admitted. Returns rendered.	
"	2		Annual Veterinary Sub post opened in conjunction with 52 M.V.S., following unity S.A.G.V.S. visited section and prevent at performance of anwermal l.o. Capt Carlisle visited section. One new admitted. Three evacuated. Two sick cases admitted.	
"	3		A.D.V.S. visited Section. Inspected horses of 5 London Field Amb. which were sent to Field Remount Depot. Two sick cases admitted. Returns rendered.	
"	4		Microscope received triplace over cook. A.D.V.S. visited Section. Four sick cases admitted. Returns rendered.	
"	5		S.A.D.V.S. visited Section. Returns rendered.	
"	6		Three sick cases admitted. One horse died, skinned & carcase buried.	

Army Form C. 2118.

WAR DIARY
INTELLIGENCE SUMMARY.
(Erase heading not required.)

Instructions regarding War Diaries and Intelligence Summaries are contained in F. S. Regs., Part II. and the Staff Manual respectively. Title pages will be prepared in manuscript.

Place	Date	Hour	Summary of Events and Information	Remarks and references to Appendices
SHEET 25 August G 32.d.9.0.	7		2 sick cases admitted. Forage received from H.Q. for shipping returned.	
"	8		Advanced veterinary aid post close through hostile shell fire. One horse over for forage for 175ft. A.D.V.S. and V.O. visited Section for enquiries. Two sick cases admitted.	
"	9		Advanced veterinary aid post working on new site. A.D.V.S. Corps & Corps Officer visited Section and examined horses fit for breeding. Horse sold for fresh for 150ft. S.C. proceeded on leave.	
"	10		Capt Bryan A.V.C. took over command of Section. Twenty three ordinary animals U.D.R case evacuated. One horse over to fresh for 175ft. Two horses admitted. Section Returns rendered.	
"	11		Capt Bryan visited Section and inspected new horses. Six sick cases admitted. Returns rendered.	

WAR DIARY
INTELLIGENCE SUMMARY.
(Erase heading not required.)

Army Form C. 2118.

Place	Date	Hour	Summary of Events and Information	Remarks and references to Appendices
SHEET 27 G 32 a 9.0	August 12		Capts Anglin & Edwards visited station. All sick horses inspected. A.D.V.S. X Corps visited station in morning afternoon three O.R. Iron sick cases admitted.	
"	13		A.D.V.S. visited station re Evacuation and moving arrangements. Nags to evacuation on arrival. One mule cast for tron fort 150 ft. kinetic sick cases admitted.	
"	14		All over cases evacuated. A.D.V.S. visited station. Section trekked to HONDINGHEM.	
WIZERNES	15		Continued trek to WIZERNES. A.D.V.S. met section and left to chair sick.	
"	16		A.D.V.S. visited section and brought Capt. MACBRIDE who took numbers of section.	
"	17		Orders received from Corp. About. Cases enrolled. Others sorrow.	
"	18			
"	19		Returns forward. No of approved on leave.	

Army Form C. 2118.

Instructions regarding War Diaries and Intelligence Summaries are contained in F. S. Regs., Part II. and the Staff Manual respectively. Title pages will be prepared in manuscript.

WAR DIARY
—of—
INTELLIGENCE SUMMARY.
(Erase heading not required.)

Place	Date	Hour	Summary of Events and Information	Remarks and references to Appendices
	August			
WIZERNES	20		Draws received from on the motor.	
"	21		Section move to KA LEULENE	
KALEULENE	22		Capt Southall C.R.E returned from leave and took command of Section. Two horse recover from civilian rities received from on the motor.	
	23		Section move to NORDEEKE	
	24		Section move to Halifax Camp.	
SHEET 2K H.B.4.9.3	25		L&R.S. visited Section. Visits and inspected horses of 520 R.E. 64/Batt Army. Twelve sick cases admitted. Returns redured.	
"	26		Lieut A.W. Smith returned from Kemmel. Visited & inspected horse of 517 & 518 Field C.R.E. Ten sick cases admitted. Returns redured.	

A6945 Wt. W14422/M1160 350,000 12/16 D. D. & L. Forms/C/2118/14.

WAR DIARY

INTELLIGENCE SUMMARY.

(Erase heading not required.)

Army Form C. 2118.

Place	Date	Hour	Summary of Events and Information	Remarks and references to Appendices
SHEET 26 August				
H 13 a 9.3	27		A.D.M.S. & A.P.M. visited Section. Visited 105 Bde & S.Infra Bath and inspected all horse Camp Horses in many places. Eight sick cases admitted.	
"	28		No horse motored and busses. First part ahead. Lt.Col. R.A.M.C. visited and inspected horse of 517, 518 & 520 Field Co. R.E. Fifteen sick cases admitted.	
"	29		Arrangements received for evacuation obviously no halts. Two cases admitted.	
"	30		Officer i/c cases evacuated. A.D.M.S. 47th Division visited 520 RE & 4th Batt. and inspected horse. Attended A.D.M.S. conference. Thirty sick cases admitted.	
"	31		Visited 517 & 518 Field Ors. R.E. inspected horses. A.D.S. II Corps visited Section re evacuation & later in the morning. Six cases admitted. Returns rendered.	

John Lowhach
Capt. A.M.C.

WA 25

CONFIDENTIAL.

WAR DIARY.

OF

1/2 LONDON MOBILE VETERINARY SECTION

FROM 1.9.17.   TO 30.9.17

Army Form C. 2118.

WAR DIARY
or
INTELLIGENCE SUMMARY.
(Erase heading not required.)

Instructions regarding War Diaries and Intelligence Summaries are contained in F. S. Regs., Part II. and the Staff Manual respectively. Title pages will be prepared in manuscript.

Place	Date	Hour	Summary of Events and Information	Remarks and references to Appendices
SHEET 27 SEPT.				
H.13.a.9.3	1		Evacuated 14 horses and 9 hides to No 23 Vety Hospl. One horse sold for slaughter for 190 francs. Horses admitted to Section 22.	
	2		Visited Field Cashier drawing pay for N.C.O.s & men. Horses admitted to Section 10.	
	3		D.A.D.V.S. visited Section. 2 other ranks proceeded on leave. Horses admitted 25. Visited G.22 d.2.4. and found suitable site for Section.	
	4		Evacuated 44 horses & 16 mules by road to No 23 Vety Hospl. 8 horses by Motor Ambulance, and 3 hides. Moved Section to G.22. d.2.4 sheet 28. Horses admitted 16. Returned to duty 3.	
SHEET 28				
G.22.D.2.4	5		D.A.D.V.S. visited the Section inspecting the cases remaining under treatment. Horses admitted 8. Returned to duty 1.	

WARY DIARY
INTELLIGENCE SUMMARY.

(Erase heading not required.)

Army Form C. 2118.

Place	Date	Hour	Summary of Events and Information	Remarks and references to Appendices
SHEET 28 G.22.D.2.4.	SEPT 6		D.A.D.V.S visited section meeting V.Os of the Division in Conference. Ten cases admitted from 37 M.V.S owing to this being full up.	
	7		Inspection of cases under treatment by D.A.D.V.S. Horses admitted 16. Returned to duty 1.	
	8		Visited the 4 Field Companies of the Division, judging on the Competition for Condition of the horses. D.A.D.V.S. would return. Horses admitted 4. Returned to duty 2.	
	9		Judges signed Competition horses in R.E. Companies. D.A.D.S. and D.D.V.S. inspected cases under treatment. Horses admitted 12. Returned to duty 1.	
	10		One case of Stomatitis discovered, causing evacuation to be suspended. D.A.D.V.S. examined all horses. 1 Horse died - Skinned and buried. Horses admitted 2. One other rank evacuated sick.	

WAR DIARY
INTELLIGENCE SUMMARY.
(Erase heading not required.)

Army Form C. 2118.

Place	Date	Hour	Summary of Events and Information	Remarks and references to Appendices
SHEET 28 G22.D24	SEPT 11		Evacuated 25 horses 9 miles by road to No 23 Vety Hosp. Visited 19 Battn London Regt. sending one case to Mobile Section for treatment. Horses admitted 6.	
	12		Visited two Companies A.S.C. and 18th Battn sending three cases to Section for evacuation. D.A.D.V.S. visited and inspected all horses under treatment. Horses admitted 5.	
	13		D.A.D.V.S. and V.Os. met at Section for Conference. Inspection the horses of 239 Machine Gun Co. admitting 2 to Mobile Section for treatment and one for evacuation. Horses admitted during day 9. One C.m. destroyed skinned and buried.	
	14		Visited 7th Battn with Capt Edwards admitting two wounded cases to Section, one for evacuation and one for treatment. One case destroyed, skinned and buried. Animals admitted 12.	

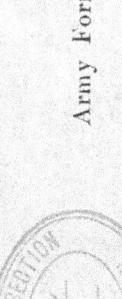

Army Form C. 2118.

WAR DIARY
— or —
INTELLIGENCE SUMMARY.
(Erase heading not required.)

SHEET 28.

Place	Date	Hour	Summary of Events and Information	Remarks and references to Appendices
G22. D.2.4.	15		D.A.D.V.S. and O.C. 3rd Australian M.V.S. visited and looked round with a view to the latter taking over from this section. Two horses destroyed skinned and buried. Visited 18th and 19th Batts and admitted 2 wounded cases one from each. Animals admitted during day 25.	
	16		Evacuated 34 horses and 10 mules by road to No 23 Vety Hospl. D.A.D.V.S and Capt. W. Brydon visited section to fix various H.Qr. for examining horses. Admitted 3.	
	17		Evacuated 5 horses and 17 mules to 1st Anzac M.V.D. Inspected 141 Machine Gun Coy horses and ordered one case to be left with 2nd Aust M.V.S. One horse admitted until oth inst.	
	18		Evacuated 4 cases to 1st Aust. M.V.S. Section moved to GODEWAERSVELDE with 19th Batt. Our HQ Dec HQ with DADVS.	

Army Form C. 2118.

WAR DIARY
of
INTELLIGENCE SUMMARY.
(Erase heading not required.)

Instructions regarding War Diaries and Intelligence Summaries are contained in F. S. Regs., Part II. and the Staff Manual respectively. Title pages will be prepared in manuscript.

Place	Date	Hour	Summary of Events and Information	Remarks and references to Appendices
GODEWAERSVELDE	19		Inspected 17th and 19th Battns with D.A.D.V.S. 2 Cold racks reinforcements arrived from No 2 Vety Hospl.	
	20		Evacuated 2 Animals to X Corps M.V.D.	
	21		Superintended entraining of 141 Machine Gun Co., Brigade H.Q. and M.V.S. at Godewaersvelde station	
LENS 11. SAVY BERLETTE	22		Section arrived Savy Berlette. Superintended detraining of horses. Marched to MAROEUIL. Occupied site allotted by Q.	
MAROEUIL	23		D.A.D.V.S. visited new site at G.1.D.8.1. sheet 51B. at present occupied by 53 M.V.S.	

A1945 Wt. W11422/M1160 350,000 12/16 D. D. & L. Forms/C/2118/14.

Army Form C. 2118.

WAR DIARY
INTELLIGENCE SUMMARY.
(Erase heading not required.)

Instructions regarding War Diaries and Intelligence Summaries are contained in F. S. Regs., Part II. and the Staff Manual respectively. Title pages will be prepared in manuscript.

Place	Date	Hour	Summary of Events and Information	Remarks and references to Appendices
MAROEUIL	24		Visited Field Cashier for pay for N.C.Os and men. Visited 4th Can. Field Amb. and made report as to unsatisfactory manner in which the shoeing was carried out, owing to their farrier Corpl. being evacuated and not replaced.	
	25		Section moved to G1.D.8.1. Took over 10 horses from 53rd M.V.S. Good accommodation for men, sheds and standings not finished. Horses admitted 11.	
SHEET 51.B. G1.D.8.1.	26		Visited new units attached – H.Q.2.H.Q., 127 Labour Co., 25 A.T.& R.E., 1st P.P.R.E. Horses admitted during day 5.	
	27		D.A.D.V.S. visited section, inspecting all cases. Visited 141 Pdn and 5th Field Amb. & Horses admitted. One other rank arrived from No 2 Vety Hospl. Completing establishment.	

Army Form C. 2118.

WAR DIARY
or
INTELLIGENCE SUMMARY.
(Erase heading not required.)

Instructions regarding War Diaries and Intelligence Summaries are contained in F. S. Regs., Part II. and the Staff Manual respectively. Title pages will be prepared in manuscript.

Place	Date	Hour	Summary of Events and Information	Remarks and references to Appendices
SHEET 51B.				
G1.D.8.1	28		Visited 4th Lond Field Amb. 239 Machine Gun Co. and 1st P.P.R.E. Met Capt Edwards and inspected 7th London Batn. ration lines. Three cases to Mobile Section for treatment. 5 Animals admitted. Returns rendered.	
	29		A.D.V.S and D.A.D.V.S visited Section and Ration lines of the M.I. Bde. pending on one case for treatment from 7th Train to Mobile Section. Admitted 7 horses. Returns Rendered	
	30		A.D.V.S. inspected Sick and Horses of Mobile Section evacuated by Motor Ambulance for slaughter. Horses admitted to Returns Rendered	

Kentish Capt A.V.C.

A6945 Wt. W14421/M1160 350000 12/16 D.D. & L. Forms/C/2118/14.

CONFIDENTIAL. WK 26

WAR DIARY

OF

1/2 London Mobile Veterinary Section.

From: 1.10.17
To: 31.10.17

Army Form C. 2118.

WAR DIARY
or
INTELLIGENCE SUMMARY.
(Erase heading not required.)

Place	Date 1917 OCT.	Hour	Summary of Events and Information	Remarks and references to Appendices
G.I.D.S.	1		A.D.V.S and D.A.D.V.S visited Section, inspecting sick horses. Held Post Mortem on horse of 5th London Field Amb. Death caused by Volvulus.	
	2		D.A.Q.M.G. and Q.P.M. inspected surplus horses ho for re-issue or section. Evacuated to No 22 Vety Hosp. 15 horses 4 mules and 7 riders. Admitted 4 cases for treatment and 2 strays. Attended 141 M.G. Co. and 20 Batts.	
	3		D.D.V.S and D.A.D.V.S called at Section inspecting horses, sheds and accommodation. Attended all units under my charge, picking on one case from 20 Batts for evacuation. A 2000's rendered. Admitted 4 cases to Section for evacuation.	
	4		Divnl Arty arrived in Area. Capt Boyden and Capt MacBrair called, the former reporting that he was sending in a suspected case of Epizootic Lymphangitis to Section. 4 cases admitted for treatment.	

Army Form C. 2118.

WAR DIARY
or
INTELLIGENCE SUMMARY.
(Erase heading not required.)

Place	Date 1917 Oct.	Hour	Summary of Events and Information	Remarks and references to Appendices
G.1 D.8.1	5		Case of Epizootic Lymphangitis admitted from No 1 Sect. D.A.C. Smears taken and forwarded to Base for verification. D.A.D.V.S. 31st and 47th Div. called and inspected the case.	
	6		D.D.V.S. and A.D.V.S. visited Section to inspect Epizootic Lymphangitis. Returns rendered. Ordered destruction and burial.	
	7		D.A.D.V.S. inspected cases remaining under treatment. Visited all Units under my charge, bringing sweepings from 2 suspected Mange cases at 141 Machine Gun Co. for microscopic examination.	
	8		Visited Units pending in cases for evacuation to Section. One case Psoroptic Mange found on case from 141 Machine Gun Co. Met D.A.D.V.S and inspected horses of Divl. Train. Five cases admitted for evacuation	

Army Form C. 2118.

WAR DIARY
or
INTELLIGENCE SUMMARY.
(Erase heading not required.)

Place	Date	Hour	Summary of Events and Information	Remarks and references to Appendices
SHEET 51C. G.1. D.81	Oct 1917			
	9		D.A.D.V.S. examined all cases for evacuation. Nineteen cases evacuated sick and five cases cast by D.D.R. Visited Machine Gun Co. 141 Bde sending in one case for evacuation. Superintended loading of sick horses at Railhead. Eleven cases admitted.	
	10		Visited all Units of 141 Bde with D.A.D.V.S. attending attached Units late in the day.	
	11		A.D.V.S and D.A.D.V.S. visited section. Inspected P.P.R.E. horses and sheds. Two strays admitted from D.A.C.	
	12		Met the V.O. of 159 Heavy Arty. R.G.A. and looked through his horses sending in three cases of mange. Inspected Drink Troughs and 20 Bn. London Regt. animals. Four cases admitted.	

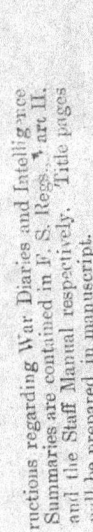

Army Form C. 2118.

WAR DIARY
or
INTELLIGENCE SUMMARY.
(Erase heading not required.)

Instructions regarding War Diaries and Intelligence Summaries are contained in F. S. Regs., Part II. and the Staff Manual respectively. Title pages will be prepared in manuscript.

Place	Date	Hour	Summary of Events and Information	Remarks and references to Appendices
SHEET 51 B G.1. D 81.13	1917 OCT. 13		D.A.D.V.S. visited Section inspecting all animals for evacuation. Ten horses and two mules evacuated to No 22 Vety. Hosp. Superintended loading of same at Railhead. Six cases admitted. Returns rendered.	
	14		A.D.V.S. called and came round to 5th London Field Amb and 1st P.P.R.E. inspecting all the animals. Three cases admitted for treatment.	
	15		Visited 141 Bde, 4 Field Ambulance inspecting all animals. Met D.A.D.V.S. and went through the horses of 20 Battn.	
	16		Met the V.O. of 48 Heavy Batty R.G.A. and went through the horses of the batty with him, sending in two cases to Section for Evacuation and one for treatment. Eight cases admitted during day.	

Army Form C. 2118.

WAR DIARY
or
INTELLIGENCE SUMMARY.
(Erase heading not required.)

Instructions regarding War Diaries and Intelligence Summaries are contained in F. S. Regs., Part II. and the Staff Manual respectively. Title pages will be prepared in manuscript.

Place	Date	Hour	Summary of Events and Information	Remarks and references to Appendices
SHEET 51B	1917 OCT			
G1.D.8.1.	17.		Divisional Commander visited Section inspecting sheds, horses and accomodation. Visited 17th Batt. London Regt. transport examining all animals. Five cases admitted for evacuation and one surplus.	
	18		D.A.D.V.S. called and accompanied me round the attached units. P.P.R.E. 25 A.T. R.E. and 139 Hy. Batty R.G.A. sending in two cases to Section.	
	19		Met D.D.R. at 47 D.A.C. lines and inspected all surplus horses and mules remaining after the new formation of the D.A.C. Stolen sent to Section for evacuation. Twenty two animals admitted during day.	
	20		D.A.D.V.S. inspected animals for evacuation, visited P.P.R.E. and 5th Lond. Field Ambulance sending in a case from each for evacuation. Evacuated thirty-six cases. Superintended loading of same at Railhead Siek animals sent to No 22 Vety. Hospl.	

Army Form C. 2118.

WAR DIARY
or
INTELLIGENCE SUMMARY.
(Erase heading not required.)

Instructions regarding War Diaries and Intelligence Summaries are contained in F. S. Regs., Part II. and the Staff Manual respectively. Title pages will be prepared in manuscript.

Place	Date	Hour	Summary of Events and Information	Remarks and references to Appendices
SHEET 51/B.	1917. OCT.			
G.1. D.8.1	21		A.D.V.S. Corps inspected Section judging in competition for prizes given by D.A.D.V.S. to best turned out Men and Horse of Section. Two Cases admitted.	
	22		Take over the 47 DAC and 47 DIVNL Train while Capt Ryder is away on Leave. Inspect the animals of 1 and 2 Co Train. Two cases admitted for evacuation.	
	23		D.D.R. inspects surplus horses of Divn that are OK for re-issue. Five sent to Section for transmission to First Army Remount Depot. Twelve animals admitted during day.	
	24		Met V.O. of 159 Heavy Batty R.G.A. going through his horses with him and pending to Section 3 cases for evacuation and 2 for treatment. Five horses sent by road to First Army Remount Depot.	

Army Form C. 2118.

WAR DIARY
or
INTELLIGENCE SUMMARY.
(Erase heading not required.)

Instructions regarding War Diaries and Intelligence Summaries are contained in F. S. Regs. Part II. and the Staff Manual respectively. Title pages will be prepared in manuscript.

[Stamp: MOBILE VETERINARY SECTION, 47th LONDON DIVISION, London, Date October 1917]

Place	Date 1917	Hour	Summary of Events and Information	Remarks and references to Appendices
SHEET 51B				
G.1 D.8.1	OCT. 25		Inspected with D.A.D.V.S. 47 D.A.C. 141 Machine Gun Co and 5th London Field Amb. Conference with D.A.D.V.S and V.Os of Units. A.2000 rendered for Units under my charge.	
	26.		A.D.V.S and D.A.D.V.S visited Section before inspecting Divisional Train. One case sent in from train for evacuation.	
	27		Selected horses for evacuation to No 22 Vety. Hosp. Superintended the loading up at Railhead. Return rendered. Evacuations notified.	
	28		Called to F Special Co. R.E. Examined case and sent Horse to Bvng to Section for treatment	

WAR DIARY
or
INTELLIGENCE SUMMARY.
(Erase heading not required.)

Army Form C. 2118.

Place	Date	Hour	Summary of Events and Information	Remarks and references to Appendices
SHEET 51.B.	1917 OCT.			
G.1.D.8.1.	29.		Met Capt. MacBride and examined sick from the animals of B.236 Batty. Sending in six animals for evacuation. Called at 18 Battn lines and sent in a case for treatment. Twelve cases admitted during day	
	30.		Visited 139 Heavy Batty R.G.A. taking scrapings from two suspected a mange cases to bring to section for microscopic examination. Proved negative. Two animals admitted to section for evacuation.	
	31.		D.A.D.V.S. called and visited 4Y.D.A.C. 141 Machine Gun Co and small attached units. Called to horse of 19th Battn, found it to be suffering from Tetanus. Admitted to section.	

CONFIDENTIAL. *VA 27*

WAR DIARY
of
1/2 London Mobile Veterinary Section.

From 1/11/17   To 30/11/17.

WAR DIARY
or
INTELLIGENCE SUMMARY.
(Erase heading not required.)

Army Form C. 2118.

1/2ND LONDON MOBILE VETERINARY SECTION

SHEET 28 NOVEMBER.

Place	Date	Hour	Summary of Events and Information	Remarks and references to Appendices
G.1. D.8.1.	1		A.D.V.S. Corps visited Section inspecting all horses under treatment. Inspected animals of 517 Field Co. 518 Field Co. and 4th Royal Welch Fusiliers. 2 horses admitted for treatment. Proceeded on Conference of V.O's to absence of D.A.D.V.S. on leave.	
"	2		Met Y.O. 1/c 4/7th R.F.A going with him through animals of the Battery, sending in to Officer in Charge and one other to Mobile Section for evacuation.	
"	3		Visited 236 Bde regarding Three debility case to Section for evacuation. 1 Congestion Lungs admitted for treatment from 518 Field Co R.E. Returns received.	
"	4		Inspected horses of P.P.R.E. 5th Lond Field Amb. and 4th Field Amb. Visited D.A.D.V.S Office to sign returns.	

A6945 Wt. W11422/M1160 350,000 12/16 D. D. & L. Forms/C./2118/14.

Army Form C. 2118.

WAR DIARY
or
INTELLIGENCE SUMMARY.
(Erase heading not required.)

1/2ND LONDON MOBILE VETERINARY SECTION

Place	Date	Hour	Summary of Events and Information	Remarks and references to Appendices
SHEET 28 C.1. D.8.1.	Nov. 5		Visited 517 and 518 Field Coys R.E. meeting D.D.R. who cast 4 animals as worn out. 15 horses admitted to section for treatment. Evacuated 22 animals to No 22 Vety Hospl.	
"	6		Met V.O. of 235 Bde and inspected A Coy pending to Austrb section 200 cases for evacuation.	
"	7		D.V.S. wired for 13 men to return to Base for transfers. Men escorted by C.O. 5th London Field Amb. Three animals admitted for treatment.	
"	8		General inspection by A.D.V.S. Corps with regard to outbreak of Mange. Interview of V.O. of D.A.D.V.S. office. 13 O.R. arrive from 2.0.10 Vety Hosps. to replace Category "A" men sent to Base for transfers.	
"	9		"A" men sent to No 2 Vety Hosp. Heart. Visited D.A.D.V.S. office regard return. Examined Gen. Goringes charger, and ordered it to section for treatment.	

WAR DIARY or INTELLIGENCE SUMMARY.

Army Form C. 2118.

12ND LONDON MOBILE VETERINARY SECTION

Place	Date	Hour	Summary of Events and Information	Remarks and references to Appendices
SHEET 28	NOVEMBER			
G.I.D.8.1.	10		A.D.V.S. Corps visited section examining all cases under treatment accompanied him to inspect the 3 Coys A.S.C. and Signal Co.	
"	11		Visited 5 Inst. Field Amb. for P.P.R.E., 18th Battn and Lt. R.W. Fusiliers sending to Mobile Section two cases supposed mange for exchange to be taken for microscopic examination.	
"	12		Inspected animals of 6th and 7th Battns and 517 Field Co. R.E. Lee Col. Edwards and examined cases and B and C Battys sending one of C135 animals to station in B.E.F. Bulletin the animals admitted during day	
"	13		Visited P.P.R.E. 1 and 3 Coys H.Q. and 21st Battn cleaning all sick cases and sending cases for evacuation to Mobile Section	
"	14		Visited the two Battns back at rest at Mount Capelle. 4.40 P.M. On horse of 1st P.P.R.E. Xtal had died during the night	

Army Form C. 2118.

WAR DIARY
or
INTELLIGENCE SUMMARY.
(Erase heading not required.)

1/2nd LONDON MOBILE VETERINARY SECTION

Place	Date	Hour	Summary of Events and Information	Remarks and references to Appendices
SHEET 28	Nov.			
G1 D.8.I.	15		Inspected all horses in Section picking out those for evacuation. Evacuated 12 cases to No. 22 Vety. Hosp. Superintended loading of horses on train at Railhead, visited H.Q. Signals and 141 M.G.Co on way back. Conference V.Os.	
"	16		D.A.D.V.S. returns from leave, visits and inspects Section. Saw 17th and 18th Divs.	
"	17		A.D.V.S. and D.A.D.V.S. visit Section inspecting all cases remaining under treatment. Inspected stabling in 22nd Batt. Accompanied A.D.V.S. 142 Bde and then to Acq. to animals admitted for treatment.	
"	18		Attended Grand Horse Show with D.A.D.V.S. Inspected 19th Battn and 2/4th D.A.C. In the afternoon visited The R.F.A. Battys at rest.	
"	19		Visited 255 M.G.Co at Frevent Capelle. Examined everything & things and passed one of 21st Battns inspects. 8 cases admitted for evacuation and evacuation.	

Army Form C. 2118.

WAR DIARY
or
INTELLIGENCE SUMMARY.
(Erase heading not required.)

1/2ND LONDON MOBILE VETERINARY SECTION

Place	Date	Hour	Summary of Events and Information	Remarks and references to Appendices
SHEET 23	NOV.			
OLD 21	20.		Hisrea 571 Leta Ant. Dur. Team sending on to section all cases unfit to travel. Saw O.C. 41 M.V.S. and arranged for him to receive all our evacuated cases.	
"	21		Evacuated all animals for evacuation and ask marching and field cases to 41 M.V.S. Orders issued for moving on 22 inst. Eleven cases admitted as unfit to travel sent to 41 M.V.S.	
"	22		Evacuated remaining cases to 41 M.V.S. Packed and moved to Dainville.	
LENS 11. DAINVILLE	23		Moved to Monchiet.	
MONCHIET	24		Rusted to Active to Bde. D.A.D.V.S. reh letter 6 P.M. and conducted on to Field allotted M.V.S. Visited other cases of 6th London Fild Amb.	

Army Form C. 2118.

WAR DIARY
or
INTELLIGENCE SUMMARY.
(Erase heading not required.)

122nd LONDON MOBILE VETERINARY SECTION

Instructions regarding War Diaries and Intelligence Summaries are contained in F. S. Regs., Part II. and the Staff Manual respectively. Title pages will be prepared in manuscript.

Place	Date	Hour	Summary of Events and Information	Remarks and references to Appendices
SHEET 57C 11				
ACHIET LE PETIT	25		D.A.D.V.S. visited Section. Two horses admitted from 2o 3 Coy Brown.	
"	26		Visited Signal Co and 10th Field Amb.	
"	27		Moved to Bapaume. D.A.D.V.S. visited Section	
Bapaume	28		Moved to N.4.B central. Four up at 2o. 14 Reserve Park - sheds and huts lent by O.C. Park. A.D.V.S. 4th Corps visited.	
SHEET 57C N.4.B central	29		Visited Mablincourt and Irecwitle with D.A.D.V.S. to pick animals vis for Sectile Section. 4 cases admitted for evacuation	
	30		Visited Achiet-le-Petit to attend 3 cases left behind by H.Q. 6th Army. Moved to Section. Evacuated 5 animals along with 41 London M.V.S. to No 9 Vety Hospl.	

[signature] Capt AVC

WAR DIARY
INTELLIGENCE SUMMARY.
(Erase heading not required.)

Army Form C. 2118.

Month Vely See
Vol 28

Place	Date	Hour	Summary of Events and Information	Remarks and references to Appendices
Bapaume	1st Dec 1917		Advanced Aid Post established at Havrincourt. 1 Offr and 2 men. Met 10 A V.O. and with him examined pack horses in section. Float sent to collect horses.	
	2nd		Two float cases collected from HQ 4 19th Batt Transport Lines. Both Officers Chargers, M.O.'s and 10 A V.O. visited section. Arrangements to move to Ruyalcourt tomorrow. Visited new area to choose site 6 Dec. Horses admitted including the 2 float cases.	
	3rd		2 Officers Chargers returned to duty. HQ section moved 15 Reinville. Later orders to Lerville to locate site for Advanced Aid Post 7 Dick. animals admitted 4 Evacuations	
Lerville	4th		Advanced Aid Post established at Termies. 1 Sgt + 2 men withdrawn from Havrincourt. Sent to Termies. 2 more were sent to Advanced Aid Post. 15 Admitted (1 Sent)	
	5th		5 Evacuations. Stretcher Advanced Aid Post destroyed by shell fire. N.CO returned whilst RAMB visited A.A. Post when first shell arrived. 1 Horse wounded from station for temporary help 6 C.C.S.	
			due & Curried. 23 Admitted (1 Horse) including 9 Gases Dermatitis. 14 Evacuated. Float sent to 5 9th M.V.S. returned	

WAR DIARY
or
INTELLIGENCE SUMMARY.

Army Form C. 2118.

(Erase heading not required.)

Place	Date	Hour	Summary of Events and Information	Remarks and references to Appendices
Neuville	6th Dec 1917		Reported to D.A.D.V.S. that Advanced Aid Post was located at Cavalry Farm.	R
"	"		Visited 140 Inf Bde. Horse lines. 9 Admitted. 10 Evacuated (2 Hosp) Advance Post visited. 1 Horse destroyed. Buried. Work at Section and Office routine.	R
"	7		On Carcass of this Section evacuated to Hospital. Work at Section and Office routine. 12 Admitted (1 Destroyed). 12 Evacuated (2 Hosp) (Dest Destroyed - both cases).	R
"	8		Had collected horse from Thiennecourt Wood 10m returned 9 a.m. following morning. Visited 14th Reserve Park A.S.C. Work at Section + Office routine. 8 Admitted. 10 Admitted.	R
"	9		Visited Advanced Aid Post. Work at Section + Office routine. 8 Admitted. 11 Evacuated.	R
"	10		Went to H.Q. 140th F.C. to collect wounded animal. Bowling raid on 140 Brigade lines. Attending horse on urgent request. 8 animals killed. 15 wounded. Visited Advanced Aid Post. Work at Section + Office routine. 13 Admitted. 15 Evacuated.	R
"	11		Went to A.123b. to collect horse. Visited Advanced Aid Post. Visited D.A.D.V.S. and conferred with him. Work at Section + Office routine. 15 Admitted. 13 Evacuated (2 Hosp).	R

Army Form C. 2118.

WAR DIARY
or
INTELLIGENCE SUMMARY.
(Erase heading not required.)

Instructions regarding War Diaries and Intelligence Summaries are contained in F.S. Regs., Part II. and the Staff Manual respectively. Title pages will be prepared in manuscript.

1/2nd LONDON F[IELD] A[MBULANCE]

Place	Date	Hour	Summary of Events and Information	Remarks and references to Appendices
Senlille	12th Nov 1917		Field Ambulance and Det[achmen]t arr[ived] on embarkation of B.E.F. really men	
			Here Work at Beeston started 140 Brigade Transport Lines. 11 Admitted	
			(Blankitis) 14 Evacuated (2 float) Float lent to 59th Div M.V.S returned.	
	13		B.O.R.S started section	
	13		Shifted 141st Reserve Park A.S.C. Not at Beeston. 4/900 forwarded	
	14		9 Admitted (5 Stomatitis collected from 6th M.V.S) 5 Evacuated	
			Not at Section Officers Latrine. Shifted 140 Brigade Transport Lines	
			13 Admitted (2 Flee) 9 Evacuated 1 Died knees	
	15		Section now being used in administration of 59th Division, A.D.V.S. 59th Div	
			Moved Section Work at Beeston Divisional Office returned. 13 Admitted 2	
			12 Evacuated	
	16		Having received Orders Section moved to Bus and Placer in relation	
			for Stomatitis Cases only Party left behind with infectious animals	
			while place prepared for their Choosing site for night 10 Admitted Present	
			6 Evacuated	
Bus	17		Shifted from Major Bus when accommodation found for Section	
			of Sick Animals. Party left behind joined Section with sick animals	
			17 Admitted	

Army Form C. 2118.

WAR DIARY
or
INTELLIGENCE SUMMARY.
(Erase heading not required.)

Instructions regarding War Diaries and Intelligence Summaries are contained in F. S. Regs., Part II. and the Staff Manual respectively. Title pages will be prepared in manuscript.

Place	Date	Hour	Summary of Events and Information	Remarks and references to Appendices
Paris	18th Dec 1914		Work at Section. Sitting place in oven. Classifying sick animals and separating them according to new plan. 33 animals admitted	
"	19	"	# M.O.'s and 26 new men from Abbeville. Shuts to avoid with sick animals. Work at Section and Office routine. Visited No 1 & 2 C.O. Du Grand 5 Armies	
"	20	"	Work at Section and Office routine. Orders received for Section to move to Meteren on 22nd inst. 6 admitted. Visited 59th A.V.S	
"	21	"	Work at Section and Office routine. Visited 59th Du D.A.V.S 2 animals. Visited No 1 Reg. 17th Du Lyons. Instructions to move tomorrow cancelled.	
"	22	"	Work at Section & Office routine. 1 admitted	
"	23	"	Work at Section & Office routine. Admissions by 17th Div	
"	24	"	Work at Section & Office routine.	
"	25	"	R.A.V.D. 17th Div. visited Section. Work at Section & Office routine.	
"	26	"	11th from A.V.S & Corps. To detail V.O. to take over charge of 24 Canes Heavy Brigade and 29th Lochan Ind. Labour Co. Visited 14th Labour Co. Work at Section.	
"	27	"	A.D.V.S + D.A.V.S 17th Division visited Section. Work at Section.	

Army Form C. 2118.

WAR DIARY
or
INTELLIGENCE SUMMARY.
(Erase heading not required.)

Instructions regarding War Diaries and Intelligence Summaries are contained in F. S. Regs., Part II. and the Staff Manual respectively. Title pages will be prepared in manuscript.

Place	Date	Hour	Summary of Events and Information	Remarks and references to Appendices
Pero	28 Decy/17		B.A.D.S & 4th Dn visited sections. Return with particulars of Stretchers	
"			Cases sent to A.D.S. Work at section of Office routine Visited B.A.D.S	Y
"	29		17th Dn at his request work returns	
"			Visited Med Coy 47th Dn Train 49th Pioneer Labour Co. Work at Office	
"	30		Section	Y
"	31		Worked Section Visited 145 Pioneer Co and 2/1 Pioneer 4.B.	
"			Worked Section Office routine Visited 236 Brigade.	

H. Fox
Capt A.V.C.
O.C. 42nd Border Mobile Veterinary Sect T.

A6945 Wt. W14422/M1160 350,000 12/16 D. D. & L. Forms/C./2118/14.

WAR DIARY
INTELLIGENCE SUMMARY.
(Erase heading not required.)

Army Form C. 2118.

1/2ND LONDON MOBILE VETERINARY SECTION

VM 29

Place	Date	Hour	Summary of Events and Information	Remarks and references to Appendices
Bus	Jany 1 1918		ADV.S. I Corps visits Section. Rules issued ADLO at Corps Head Quarters. Work at Section. Instructions for Out of Bounds horses to be picked up suggested by ADVS	
	2		DADVS. 17th Division visits Section. Inspected animals. Work at Section	
	3		Visits 145 Labour Co. and 5 Cheshire Labour Co. Attending 19 ADVS	
	4		at his Office. Office Routine. Work at Section. ADVS I Corps to visit Section. Report sent to ADVS 47th Division as requested with reference to General Goringe's horse. Work at Section. Office Routine.	
	5		H.R.N. & horse discharged to duty unit. Visits No1 Cav. 47th Div. Train. Worked at Section & Office Routine	
	6		One Case Pneumatitis, belonging to 135 Hy Bde R.G.A. admitted. Work at Section & Office Routine	
	7		47th Division resumed administration of this Section. Visits 235 Brigade R.F.A. Work at Section and Office Routine	
	8		Inspected animals at Hq D.A. Work at Section and	

* Army Form C. 2118.

WAR DIARY
or
INTELLIGENCE SUMMARY.
(Erase heading not required.)

1/2ND LONDON MOBILE VETERINARY SECTION

Instructions regarding War Diaries and Intelligence Summaries are contained in F. S. Regs., Part II. and the Staff Manual respectively. Title pages will be prepared in manuscript.

Place	Date	Hour	Summary of Events and Information	Remarks and references to Appendices
Bra	Jany 8 1918		Office routine.	
	9		Inspecting Remounts of 235th Brigade R.F.A. Report thereon sent to O.C. Visited No4 Coy 47th Divn Train. Instruction re men chosen for Sergeants A.V.C. work at section office routine.	
	10		Visited No1 Coy A.S.C. Getting out Returns A/1000. Attending Conference at Office of D.A.D.V.S. 9 le guards to 48 C.C.S. by M.O. work at section & office routine.	
	11		Visited No1 Coy A.S.C. Report to D.A.D.V.S. that cases of Ringworm had appeared in animals isolated in this section. Work at section. Office routine. Similar instruction to men as above	
	12		Visited 520th Field Co R.E. Attending Field Cashier. Paid NCOs & men. Work at Section & Office routine.	
	13		Visited 6th London Field Ambulance. Work at section Office routine. Sgt Walker Ae Anglice proceeded on leave. Work at section & Office routine.	
	14		Visited No1 Coy A.S.C. Work at Section and Office routine.	

A6945 Wt. W14422/M160 350,000 12/16 D. D. & L. Forms/C./2118/14.

Army Form C. 2118.

1/2ND LONDON MOBILE VETERINARY SECTION

No. ....
Date ....

WAR DIARY
or
INTELLIGENCE SUMMARY.

(Erase heading not required.)

Instructions regarding War Diaries and Intelligence Summaries are contained in F. S. Regs., Part II. and the Staff Manual respectively. Title pages will be prepared in manuscript.

Place	Date	Hour	Summary of Events and Information	Remarks and references to Appendices
Bus	Jany 15th 1918		Visited Nos 2, 3 +4 Corps A.D.C. Worked Section and Office routine. D.A.D.V.S. 7th Division visited Section.	
"	16		Visited 145th Labour Co. +166 Labour Co, 42 +1st Labour Co. +294th Coys Labour. Enq. Labour Co. Work of Section + Office routine	
"	17		Preparing A/2000. Attended Conference of V.Os at office of D.A.D.V.S. Visited 5th London Field Ambulance + Nos 1. 2. 3. +4 Coys. A/745 Div.	
"	18		Ivm. Work at Section + Office routine. D.A.D.V.S. 47th Div. visited Section - Visited 5th London Field Amb.	
"	19		Work at Section + office routine. Losses Army L.D. Bay Co. to 255th M.G.C. D.A.D.V.S. visited Section, Work at Section - Visited No 2 Co. A.S.C.	
"	20		Visited 5th London Field Ambulance - Work at Section + Office routine	
"	21		Worked Nos 3 +4 Corps A.D.C. 18th Battn London Regt +5th 18th Field Co. R.E. D.A.D.V.S. visited Section. Work at Section + Office routine. 9h.	
"	22		D.A.D.V.S. visited Section (Proceeded on leave). Visited 15/23rd Bn. +1/236 Bn, R.H.A. +181st Battn London Regt. Returned 12 Mules A/6 Nos 2, 3 +4 Corps A.D.C.	

WAR DIARY
or
INTELLIGENCE SUMMARY.
(Erase heading not required.)

Army Form C. 2118.

1/2ND LONDON MOBILE VETERINARY SECTION
No....................
Date..................

Place	Date	Hour	Summary of Events and Information	Remarks and references to Appendices
Bus	Jany 22 1918		horses to duty subject to 14 days isolation by Vint. Work at Section + Office routine.	
	23		Visited No 1+2 Corps MDS, 678 Field Co R.E. 700th Labour Co 45 K. London Field Ambulance. Work at Section + Office routine	
			Issued Pony to D. Coy May to 518 Field Co R.E. 29 horses returned to duty free from Promotitis subject to 14 days isolation by Vint.	
	24		Preparing A/200s. Attended Conference of V.Os at Office of D.A.D.V.S. Work at Section + Office routine 1 Riem B[r].M. abandoned to 140 B.T.O.	
	25		Visited No 204 Corps MDS. Pte Bamsley sent to Base for A.V.C. Depot Course. Work at Section + Office routine.	
	26		19.19 R. visited Section to inspect Revenors Cases. S.G. S.V. 2 marked Section. Work at Section + Office routine.	
	27		D.A.D.V.S. visited Section. Pte Jones admitted to Field Ambulance. Visited 2/c Convoy Field Ambulance Horse Lines. Work at Section	
	28		Visited 518 Field Co R.E. who 3 Cav MSC. Sgt Cheetle proceeds on 3 days Catering Course. Work at Section + Office routine.	

WAR DIARY
or
INTELLIGENCE SUMMARY.
(Erase heading not required.)

Army Form C. 2118.

1/2ND LONDON MOBILE VETERINARY SECTION

Place	Date	Hour	Summary of Events and Information	Remarks and references to Appendices
Bus.	Jany 29 1918		On Parade as usual. Visited Field Cashier. Sent N.C.O's men. Visited No 1 & Corps A.D. Work at Section. One animal discharges to duty free from Dermatitis subject to 14 days isolation by mud. D.A.D.V.S. visited Section. D.A.D.V.S. 74th Div visited Section. Pte Hughes returned from leave.	
	30		On hitting processes to Abbeville for Course of Farriery. 5 Animals discharged to duty free from Dermatitis subject to 14 days isolation by mud. Work at Section. Office routine. Visited 3rd & 4th Bgde A.S.C. Preparing A.F.B. 200. Attending Conference of V.O's at Office of D.A.D.V.S. D.A.D.V.S. visited Section. A.D.V.S. Corps rabies Section. Pte Thursby proceeded on leave. One animal discharged to duty free from Dermatitis subject to isolation by Muck 10 Camer Tuy. Work at Section. Office routine. Visited 42nd, 145 Bn & 291st Archan Ind Labour Co.	
	31			

K. K...
Capt. A.V.C.
O.C. 1/2nd London Mobile Veterinary Section
47th Division.

Army Form C. 2118.

WAR DIARY
or
INTELLIGENCE SUMMARY.
(Erase heading not required.)

1/2ND LONDON MOBILE VETERINARY SECTION

Place	Date	Hour	Summary of Events and Information	Remarks and references to Appendices
Bruay	February 1	1918	D.A.D.V.S. visited Section. Pte Cheale returned from Quivering Course. Visited Nos 1 & 2 Coy. Div. Train. Work at Section. Office routine	
"	2		D.D.V.S & D.A.D.V.S. visited Section. Visited 5th London Field Ambulance. Dy Walden returned from leave. Pte Wigg proceeded on leave. Work at Section. Office routine	
"	3		D.A.D.V.S. visited Section. Visited 2.53rd Machine Gun Co. & 518 Field Co. R.E. Work at Section. Office routine	
"	4		D.V.S., D.D.V.S. A.D.V.S. and D.A.D.V.S. with American Visitors inspected Section. O.C. proceeded on leave. Pte Field proceeded on leave. Capt. Edwards A.V.C. appointed acting O.C. of Section	
"	5		D.A.D.V.S. visited Section. Visited 04.9.13th Bde. R.F.A., 6th London Field Ambulance, 18th Battalion London Regt, 236 Bde. R.F.A., Div. Arty. H.Q. Work at Section	
"	6		M.V.S. opened to receive cases. Visited D.A.A. Section D.A.C. B.236. A.236 Bde. R.F.A. Pte Griffith joined Section as reinforcement. Work at Section. Preparing Returns &/2000. Attending Conference at Office of DADVS.	
"	7		Visited 236 Bde R.F.A. & D.A.C. Section of DAC. Pte Guigh proceeded on leave. Work at Section	

Army Form C. 2118.

WAR DIARY
or
INTELLIGENCE SUMMARY.
(Erase heading not required.)

1/2ND LONDON MOBILE VET.y SECTION

Place	Date	Hour	Summary of Events and Information	Remarks and references to Appendices
Bus	1918 Feby 8		Inspected Remounts. Visited 23rd & 24th Battalions, 141 and 142 Machine Gun Cos. Div. Arty. H.Q. & 186 Battn. D.A.D.V.S. visited Section. Sgt. Carey of 22nd Battalion attached to Section to give instruction in Mokohy work at Section. Office routine	
"	9		O/c Neale proceeded on leave. Visited 22nd Battn. & 141 Brigade (18th, 19th, 20th Battns.) & H.Q. 142 Inf. Bde. M.V.D. closed for ordinary cases. 11 animals evacuated. 77 Remounts admitted for isolation (+ domestic)	
"	10		Visited 19th, 20th, 21st Battalions, 141 Machine Gun Co. A/236 & B/236 Bde. R.F.A. & D.A.C. Section. Work at Section & Office routine.	
"	11		Work at Section and Office routine	
"	12		Visited 17th, 19th, 23rd & 24th Battalions. 13/236 & H.Q.236. A.D.V.S. visited Section. Work at Section and Office routine.	
"	13		Visited 255 Machine Gun Co. & 4th Royal Welsh Fusiliers & 141 Machine Gun Co. Work at Section & Office routine	
"	14		Preparing A/2000. Visited 236 Brigade R.F.A. and Field Cashier. Attended Conference of V.Os at OA.D.V.S. Office. Work at Section & Office routine	

WAR DIARY

INTELLIGENCE SUMMARY

Army Form C. 2118.

1/2ND LONDON MOBILE VETERINARY SECTION

Place	Date	Hour	Summary of Events and Information	Remarks and references to Appendices
Bruay				
Feby.	15	1918	Visited 23rd Brigade R.F.A. & D.A.C. Section D.A.C. Visited Field Cashier. Work at Section & Office routine.	
	16		Visited 2nd London Field Ambulance, 236 Bde R.F.A. & Field Cashier. Sgt. N.C.O. i/men of Section. Work at Section – Office routine.	
	17		The Ward sent to be attached to Army M.V.D. Pte Landy returned from leave. Visited 142 Inf Bde (2nd & 17th Battns) 17th Battn 1/42 Machine Gun Co. Work at Section & Office routine.	
	18		D.A.D.V.S. visited Section. Work at Section & Office routine.	
	19		Visited 255 Machine Gun Co., 4th Royal Welsh Fusiliers, 1/41 Inf Bde H.Q. & 1st London Field Ambulance. Pte Wiggs returned from leave. Worked Section. Visited 236 Bde R.F.A. Work at Section. 5 Animals returned to Units.	
	20		O.C. returned from leave. Cpl Ross & Pte Murphy proceeded on leave. Sgmr Gifford proceeded on leave for one month. Pioneering A/2000 attending Conference of V.Os at Office of D.A.D.V.S. 66 animals returned to Units	
	21		D.A.D.V.S. visited Section. Visited 5th London Field Ambulance and	
	22		C.L.D.V Corps. Work at Section & Office/routine. Report on Inner Billy Horse Shoe Road rendered	

Army Form C. 2118.

WAR DIARY
INTELLIGENCE SUMMARY.
(Erase heading not required.)

1/2ND LONDON MOBILE VETERINARY SECTION

Instructions regarding War Diaries and Intelligence Summaries are contained in F. S. Regs., Part II. and the Staff Manual respectively. Title pages will be prepared in manuscript.

Place	Date	Hour	Summary of Events and Information	Remarks and references to Appendices
Bus	1918			
	February 23		D.A.D.V.S. visited Section. Visited 5th London Field Ambulance, Nos 1,2,3 & 4 Coy. Div. Train. Work at Section & Office routine.	
	24		Visited Div. Gas Officer and work with A.D.V.S. to A.P.V.O.I. Corps. Work at Section. Office routine.	
	25		D.A.D.V.S. visited Section. Visited Field Cashier. Paid N.C.O. & men of Section. Work at Section & Office routine.	
	26		Div. Gas N.C.O. examines all Box Respirators in Section. Visited Nos 2, 3 & 4 Coy. Div. Train, 6R, 7R, 8R, 15th & 24th Inf. Battns, 140 Bde H.Q., 517, 518, 519, 520 Field A.R.S. & 9 & 2 M.G. & 7th D.W. Work at Section. Pte Leigh returned from leave.	
	27		Visited 4th & 5th London Field Ambulances & 1/5 Royal W. Kent workers. Work at Section & Office Routine.	
	28		D.A.D.V.S. visited Section. Remounts for Division arrived at M.V.S. & examined. Preparing tendering A/2000. Attended Conference of V.Os. at Office of D.A.D.V.S. Work at Section. Office routine. Pte Neale returned from leave.	

Gloucester

Capt. A.V.C.

O.C. 1/2nd London Mobile Veterinary Section

29

4.4.18

To
D.A.D.V.S.
47 London Div.

Herewith please receive
WAR DIARY
of this Section
for month ending 31. 3. 18.

J Craig Capt. A.V.C.
Cmd. 1/2 London M.V.S.

CONFIDENTIAL

WAR DIARY. OF

1/2 London Mobile Veterinary Section

From 1/3/18

To 31/3/18.

WAR DIARY
or
INTELLIGENCE SUMMARY.

(Erase heading not required.)

Army Form C. 2118.

Place	Date	Hour	Summary of Events and Information	Remarks and references to Appendices
SHEET 57c. O.24.c.	MARCH			
	1		Visited 517 Field Co. R.E. Destroyed H.D. suffering from fractured Radius. 518 and 520 Field Cos. Rifle Ranges witnesses firing practice. Divisional Commander visited Section.	
	2		Horse admitted from 6th London Field Amb. suspected case of Enzootic Lymphangitis. Smears taken. Result negative. O.C. 19 Divn. M.V.S. visited Section.	
	3		Inspected Horses of 18th and 19th Batts. and 141 Bde Head Quarters. D.D.V.S. and O.C. 6th London Field Amb. visited Section.	
	4		Newly arrived N.C.O. & Driver reported for duty to Division. D.D.V.S. and D.A.D.V.S. visited Section.	
	5		Visited 517, 518 & 520 Field Cos. R.E. Visited Field Cashier. Visited R.W.F. and destroyed animal suffering from fractured humerus.	

Army Form C. 2118.

WAR DIARY
or
INTELLIGENCE SUMMARY.
(Erase heading not required.)

Instructions regarding War Diaries and Intelligence Summaries are contained in F. S. Regs., Part II. and the Staff Manual respectively. Title pages will be prepared in manuscript.

Place	Date	Hour	Summary of Events and Information	Remarks and references to Appendices
SHEET 57c O.24.c.	6		Years sent to 517 Field Co. RE to collect case. Visited 2, 3 & 4 Coss D.S.C. also 51 Field Amb and M.O. of Bde. The prescribed weekly course fixed in presence of Staff Officer	
	7		Tour pack cases admitted to isoln. Returns rendered. Attended Conference in afternoon.	
	8		Five cases evacuated to British Evacuation Station. D A D V S visited. Lecture. Visited 51 London Field Amb.	
	9		Divisional Gymkana O.C's charge visits after Steeple chase. Returns rendered.	
	10		Met D.A.D.V.S. and Inspected horses of Nos 1 & 2 Co. Divisional train. Return rendered	

Army Form C. 2118.

WAR DIARY
or
INTELLIGENCE SUMMARY.
(Erase heading not required.)

Instructions regarding War Diaries and Intelligence Summaries are contained in F. S. Regs., Part II. and the Staff Manual respectively. Title pages will be prepared in manuscript.

Place	Date	Hour	Summary of Events and Information	Remarks and references to Appendices
SHEET 57C O.24.C.	March 11		Visited and Inspected annexes of 517, 518 & 520 Field Coy R.E. No cases admitted. No Tn. Section. Two O.R. returned from leave	
	12		Eight sick cases admitted. Visited Transport of 140 Bde.	
	13		D.A.D.V.S. visited Section and inspected horses for evacuation. Further cases evacuated to Corps V.E.S. Three sick cases admitted	
	14		Three sick cases admitted. Returned visit of Visiting Officer of V.O. at D.Q. & V.S. office in afternoon	
	15		Visited 140 Inf. Bde. and went to Horse Section 3 cases for evacuation Returns rendered	

WAR DIARY
or
INTELLIGENCE SUMMARY.
(Erase heading not required.)

Army Form C. 2118.

Place	Date	Hour	Summary of Events and Information	Remarks and references to Appendices
SHEET 57C. O. 24. C	March 16		D.A.D.V.S. visited Station Second Divisional Gymkana - assisted.	
			Returns rendered	
	17		Eight cases evacuated to Corps V.E.S. Four pick cases admitted	
			Returns rendered	
	18		Visited 517 - 518 & 520 Field Coy R.E. Four pick cases admitted. HeTanus	
			Case admitted on 2a. inst destroyed	
	19		Ten cases admitted. D.A.D.V.S. inspection cases in Lines for evacuation	
			Twelve cases evacuated to Corps Vety Evacuation Station	
	20		Poor part. Ic colonel met from Divil H.Q. also from M.A. Bath Day	
			Cases evacuated to Corps V.E.S. Six cases admitted for treatment	

Army Form C. 2118.

WAR DIARY
or
INTELLIGENCE SUMMARY.
(Erase heading not required.)

Instructions regarding War Diaries and Intelligence Summaries are contained in F. S. Regs., Part II. and the Staff Manual respectively. Title pages will be prepared in manuscript.

Place	Date	Hour	Summary of Events and Information	Remarks and references to Appendices
SHEET 57c.				
O.26.c.	21		Three cases evacuated by Mort. from Signal Co. to Corps V.E.S. Advanced Ad. Post established. 1 N.C.O. 2 men. Attended Conference of V.Os at D.A.D.V.S office.	
"	22		Camp shelled. Horses taken out into fields.	
"	23		Return to Guillemont. O.C. thrown from horse - injured.	
GUILLEMONT	24		Return to Bernancourt. O.C. admitted to Hospital - evacuated.	
BERNANCOURT	25		Col. MacBride in charge of Section moved to Foisseaux and Mita to Warloy	
WARLOY	26		Moved to Vauchelles with Personnel Train.	
VAUCHELLES	27		Moved with Div. Train to Buchvillers. Capt Craig AVC. Reported as O.C. DADVS voucher.	

Army Form C. 2118.

WAR DIARY
or
INTELLIGENCE SUMMARY.
(Erase heading not required.)

Instructions regarding War Diaries and Intelligence Summaries are contained in F. S. Regs., Part II. and the Staff Manual respectively. Title pages will be prepared in manuscript.

Place	Date	Hour	Summary of Events and Information	Remarks and references to Appendices
HENS II MAP	MARCH			
PUCHEVILLERS	28		Two sick cases admitted for treatment	
"	29		Moved to SEPTENVILLE. Three cases admitted	
SEPTENVILLE	30		D.A.D.V.S. visited. Nine cases admitted	
"	31		Two cases admitted. Seven cases admitted to VII Corps V.E.S. Returns rend.	

J. Craig Capt avr to

WAR DIARY
INTELLIGENCE SUMMARY.
(Erase heading not required.)

Army Form C. 2118.

Place	Date	Hour	Summary of Events and Information	Remarks and references to Appendices
Septonville April	1	1918	Pte Nelan returned from 5/16 London Field Ambulance - 10 Animals admitted - 9 Evacuated - Work at Section and Office routine.	
	2		Visited 2, 3 + 4 Cos. Div Train - Inspected 141 Brigade - 5 Animals admitted 9 Evacuated - Work at Section and Office routine.	
	3		Inspected 142 Brigade and R.E. 8 Animals admitted - Driver Sifford returned from 1 month's leave. Work at Section.	
	4		Visited 2, 3 + 4 Co. Div Train - Visited D.A.D.V.S. at his Office - Prepared and rendered returns A/1000 - Horse sent to Railhead. Work at Section - 1 Admitted 10 Evacuated	
	5		Visited 2, 3 + 4 Co. Div Train - Visited D.A.D.V.S. Inspected Remounts at Richerbillers - Posted advanced Aid Post at Warloy (1 N.C.O. and 3 men) 5 P.M. Work at Section - 2 Admitted.	
	6		Visited 140 Brigade, 142 Brigade, M.G. Battalion + R.E. Visited Aid Post - Work at Section - 9 Admitted	
	7		Work at Section - 3 Admitted - 12 Evacuated. Pte Aylott returned from leave	
	8		Inspected No 3 Co. Div Train. Visited Aid Post. Work at Section - 2 Admitted 5 Evacuated	

WAR DIARY
INTELLIGENCE SUMMARY
(Erase heading not required.)

Army Form C. 2118.

Vol. 32

Place	Date	Hour	Summary of Events and Information	Remarks and references to Appendices
Pernonille	April 9	1918	Section moved to Val de Maison. D.A.D.V.S. visited Section - Aid Post withdrawn. Work at Section - 1 Admitted.	
Val de Maison	April 10	"	D.A.D.M.S. visited Section - Visited 141 Brigade, 142 Brigade and 518th C.R.E. Work at Section - 5 Reinforcements arrived from Base Hospital.	
	11		5 Animals admitted. New Ford collected from Railhead. Prepared and rendered Return A/2000. Work at Section. 1 Admitted.	
			4 Section Section received orders to move. Part of journey done when further orders received to return.	
	12		Section moved to Bt. Hilaire - Visited 5th London Field Ambulance. Visited D.A.D.V.S. to report. Work at Section.	
	13		Section moved to Domvast - All day on road.	
Domvast	14		Visited No 3 Co. Div. Train - Work at Section.	
	15		Visited 517th Co. F.S. 201st Co. R.E. No. 9 Battalion and 5th London Field Amb. D.A.D.V.S. visited Section - Visited Pack French horse at Hellincourt Farm - Work at Section - 1 Admitted.	
	16		Visited 141 Brigade H.Q., No 3 Co. Div. Train, 19th Battalion and 5 L. London	

Army Form C. 2118.

WAR DIARY
INTELLIGENCE SUMMARY.
(Erase heading not required.)

Instructions regarding War Diaries and Intelligence Summaries are contained in F. S. Regs., Part II. and the Staff Manual respectively. Title pages will be prepared in manuscript.

Place	Date	Hour	Summary of Events and Information	Remarks and references to Appendices
Donnrast				
April	16	1918	Field Ambulance. Work at Dechon – 1 Admitted.	
	17		Visited HK Royal Welsh Fusiliers, 18th Battalion & 20th Battalion. Work at Dechon – 3 Admitted.	
	18		Visited 18th Battalion and 20th Battalion. Prepared and rendered returns. A/2000. Attended Conference of VOs at Office of DADVS. Work at Dechon. 6 Admitted. 9 Prepared.	
	19		Visited No 3 Co Div Transport 5th London Field Ambulance. Work at Dechon. 4 Admitted. 2 Category despatched to No 2 Veterinary Hospital	
	20		Visited 18th Battn and 47th M.G. Battalion. Work at Dechon.	
	21		ADVX Corps and DADVD visited Dechon. Work at Dechon.	
	22		Visited 141 Brigade HQ, 19th Battalion and HL R.W.F. Work at Dechon. 10 Evacuated – (1 Horse)	
	23		Visited 18th London Batt. and No 3 Co Div Trans. Work at Dechon. 4 admitted.	
	24		Visited 4th Royal Welsh Fusiliers. Inspected Remounts and reported hereon to DADVS. – 1 Admitted.	
	25		Visited 18th & 20th Battalions. Prepared A/2000 and attended Conference of	

Army Form C. 2118.

WAR DIARY
— or —
INTELLIGENCE SUMMARY.
(Erase heading not required.)

Instructions regarding War Diaries and Intelligence Summaries are contained in F. S. Regs., Part. II. and the Staff Manual respectively. Title pages will be prepared in manuscript.

Place	Date	Hour	Summary of Events and Information	Remarks and references to Appendices
Domvast	April 25	1918	V.Os at Office of D.A.D.V.S. Work at Section - 4 Admitted.	
	26		Visited D.A.D Section 47th D.A.C. Inspected No 3 Co. 47th Div Train. Work at	
			Section. 4 Evacuated. Two men sent to No 2 Vty Hospl. on 9th inst	
			returned marked Category B1 and B2 respectively. D.A.D.V.S. visited	
	27.		Section. 1 Admitted. 5th London Field Ambulance & 20th Battalion - D.A.D.V.S visited	
			Section D.D.V.S. Inspected Section. Worked. Section. 7 Admitted 3 Evacuated.	
	28		(Cy Scot) Sic Robertson Category A man sent to No 2 Veterinary Hospital.	
			Work at Section. Sleeping by awaiting orders to move.	
	29		7 Admitted. 8 Evacuated.	
			Section moved to Brucamps. Work at Section. 1 Evacuated.	
Brucamps	30		Section moved to Allonville. All day on road.	

J Craig Capt. A.V.C.
O.C. 1/2nd London M.V.S.

47

CONFIDENTIAL

WR 33

WAR DIARY

of

1/2nd London Mobile Vety. Section.

From 1/5/18   To 31.5.18.

Army Form C. 2118.

WAR DIARY
or
INTELLIGENCE SUMMARY.
(Erase heading not required.)

1/2ND LONDON MOBILE VETERINARY SECTION
No. ....
Date. May 1918

Place	Date	Hour	Summary of Events and Information	Remarks and references to Appendices
	MAY			
Allonville	1		Visited Vets R.V. & No 3 Coy Divnl Train 5th Divisn Field Amb. and inspected horses	
			Received orders to move Section on 2nd tomorrow	
Beaucourt	2		Section moved to Beaucourt taking over from 2nd Australian Mv.V.S. 18 sick cases admitted	
	3		D.A.D.V.S. visited Section. Attended board to pass shoeing smiths. 9 sick cases admitted	
	4		D.A.D.V.S. visited Section and inspected 23 cases for Evacuation. Visited by invitation to U.S. Engineers and inspected horses. 2 sick cases admitted. Returns rendered.	
	5		D.A.D.V.S. visited Section. Visited and inspected 4 Coy Train and 5th Field Ambulance. A.D.V.S. Australian Corps visited and inspected Section. 49 sick cases admitted.	

Army Form C. 2118.

12ND
LONDON MOBILE
VETERINARY SECTION
to ....
Date May 1918

WAR DIARY
or
INTELLIGENCE SUMMARY.
(Erase heading not required.)

Instructions regarding War Diaries and Intelligence Summaries are contained in F. S. Regs., Part II. and the Staff Manual respectively. Title pages will be prepared in manuscript.

Place	Date	Hour	Summary of Events and Information	Remarks and references to Appendices
	MAY			
Bruscourt	6		D.A.D.V.S. visited and inspected 50 cases for evacuation. Visits and inspected Horse lines 152nd & 153rd Bgs. Div. Train. 25 sick cases admitted	
	7		D.A.D.V.S. visited and inspected 26 cases for evacuation. Visited Portland Sick Amb and inspected horses. 4 sick cases admitted. 1 horse destroyed, skinned & carcase buried	
	8		Visited Field Bakery and opened Supervist etc. Visited and inspected horses of H.Q. 141 Inf. Bgde. 181st 191st 90th Batts. London Rgts. 24 sick cases evacuated 24 sick cases admitted	
	9		D.A.D.V.S. visited and inspected 62 cases for evacuation. D.D.V.S. III Corps visited and inspected section. 66 sick cases admitted. 1 Lieut, 1 Sergt 1 NCO and one bird Returns rendered	
	10		Visited & inspected horses of 442 Fors. Field Amb. 17 sick cases admitted	

Army Form C. 2118.

1/2ND LONDON MOBILE VETERINARY SECTION
No. ....
Date May 1918

WAR DIARY
or
INTELLIGENCE SUMMARY.
(Erase heading not required.)

Place	Date	Hour	Summary of Events and Information	Remarks and references to Appendices
Beaucourt	MAY 11		D.A.D.V.S. visited and inspected 12 sick cases for evacuation. Visited and inspected horses of 3 Coy Divl Train. H.Q 141 Inf Bde 18th 19th & 20th Battns London Regt. 124 sick cases admitted. Returns rendered.	
	12		Fort Rest to H.Q Bde. to collect wounded horses. 5 Cases admitted	
	13		Visited and inspected horses of 140 Inf Bde H.Q 15th 17th 18th 19th and Div Battns London Regt. 9 sick cases admitted. 1 destroyed. Shinned oil carcase buried.	
	14		D.A.D.V.S visited section and inspected 21 sick cases for evacuation. Visited A.D.V.S Field Amb. & 3 Coy Divl Train. 8 sick cases admitted.	
	15		D.A.D.V.S. visited section and inspected 10 sick cases for evacuation. Visited and inspected horses of 141 Inf Bde. 142nd Bde & Divl Cn. & D.A.D.V.S office. Returns rendered. 15 sick cases admitted	

Army Form C. 2118.

1/2ND LONDON MOBILE VETERINARY SECTION
No. Army Form 8
Date............

WAR DIARY
or
INTELLIGENCE SUMMARY.
(Erase heading not required.)

Instructions regarding War Diaries and Intelligence Summaries are contained in F. S. Regs., Part II. and the Staff Manual respectively. Title pages will be prepared in manuscript.

Place	Date	Hour	Summary of Events and Information	Remarks and references to Appendices
	MAY			
Beaucourt	16		D.A.D.V.S. visited and inspected 10 sick cases for evacuation. Visited 4th Fd. Field Amb. and to 3 Coy Durl. L.I. Own 1 destroyed skinned and carcase buried. 15 sick cases admitted	
"	17		D.A.D.V.S. visited and inspected 9 cases for evacuation. Visited 517 518 and 520 Field Coys R.E. also 14th R.W.F. Also surplus O.R. sent to 80 F.Y.E.S. by actn of A.D.V.S. III Corps. Two animals been attacked by Horse. 13 sick cases admitted	
"	18		D.A.D.V.S. visited and inspected 17 cases for evacuation. Visited and inspected 4th London Fd. Amb. and 7th attached Labour Coy. 17 sick cases admitted	
"	19.		Visited and inspected 141 Bde H.Q. 18th 19th & 20th Battns. 6 cases adm. ett.	
"	20		D.A.D.V.S. visited and inspected 13 cases for evacuation. 1 wounded case collected. 1 destroyed skinned and buried. 5 cases ad.mitted. Visited Field Cashier - Returns rendered.	

Army Form C. 2118.

1/2ND LONDON MOBILE VETERINARY SECTION
No. May 1918
Date

WAR DIARY
or
INTELLIGENCE SUMMARY.
(Erase heading not required.)

Instructions regarding War Diaries and Intelligence Summaries are contained in F.S. Regs., Part II. and the Staff Manual respectively. Title pages will be prepared in manuscript.

Place	Date	Hour	Summary of Events and Information	Remarks and references to Appendices
Beaucourt	MAY 21		D.A.Q.M.G. and D.P.M. visited section. Visited and inspected 2/o 3 Coy. Train and 5th Lond. Field Amb. 17 sick cases admitted. N.C.Os and men paid.	
	22		D.A.D.V.S. visited and inspected 26 cases for evacuation. Visited and inspected 42nd & 51st Div. Fld. Ambs and 3 Coy Divl Train. Minor Operations performed at D.A.D.V.S. office. 8 sick cases admitted.	
	23		D.A.D.V.S. visited and inspected sick cases remaining under treatment. Visited and inspected 35th Labour Groups and 256 Tunnelling Co R.E. 14 sick cases admitted.	
	24		D.A.D.V.S. visited and inspected 14 cases for evacuation. 1 destroyed. Horses and car cases issued. Visited 3 Coy Divl Train. Batta Sub Parks & Bearers. invalid picquet. 2 sick cases admitted.	

A6945 Wt. W14422/M1160 350,000 12/16 D. D. & L. Forms/C/2118/14.

Army Form C. 2118.

WAR DIARY
or
INTELLIGENCE SUMMARY.
(Erase heading not required.)

1/2ND LONDON MOBILE VETERINARY SECTION
May 1918

Place	Date	Hour	Summary of Events and Information	Remarks and references to Appendices
	MAY			
Beaucourt	25		Visited and inspected 2 Coy Iron and 141 Feld A.Q. 182 H.A. & Sect. Bn Tr. Strong Point. Admitted 1 sick case.	
"	26		D.A.D.V.S. visited and inspected 16 pack animals for evacuation. Visited with D.A.D.V.S. O.P. inspected horses of D.H.Q, D.A.C as Appx & R.E. 2 sick cases admitted.	
"	27		Visited and inspected S.H.Corps Field Pens. 4th Cav. A.H.T. and 250 Sqn. Coy R.E. 16 sick cases admitted. 1 O.R. attached to Section as Sh... for duties.	
"	28		F.A.D.V.S. visited and inspected 10 sick cases for evacuation to horse Bath. 7 sick cases admitted.	
"	29		D.A.D.V.S. visited and inspected 13 cases for evacuation 1 sh... to horse D.A.D.V.S. visited & in... ... S.V.O. attended. 12 sick cases ...	

Army Form C. 2118.

WAR DIARY
or
INTELLIGENCE SUMMARY.
(Erase heading not required.)

1/2ND LONDON MOBILE VETERINARY SECTION
No.
Date. May 1918

Place	Date	Hour	Summary of Events and Information	Remarks and references to Appendices
	MAY.			
Beaucourt	30		Visits and inspection animals of 141 Bde H.Q. 187th Bde and 20th Bns.	
			1. Collected by float. 1 sick case admitted	
	31		D.A.D.V.S. visited and inspected. 1½ cases for evacuation. Inspection	
			236 Jun Coy R.E. 10 sick cases admitted Nine rendered	

J Craig Capt. AVC
Cmd ½ Section MVS

47

96/34

WAR DIARY

OF

1/2 London Mobile Veterinary Section

From June 1st 1918
To June 30th 1918.

Confidential

Army Form C. 2118.

WAR DIARY
or
INTELLIGENCE SUMMARY.
(Erase heading not required.)

1/2ND LONDON MOBILE VETERINARY SECTION
No. 1
Date June 1918

Instructions regarding War Diaries and Intelligence Summaries are contained in F. S. Regs., Part II. and the Staff Manual respectively. Title pages will be prepared in manuscript.

Place	Date	Hour	Summary of Events and Information	Remarks and references to Appendices
	JUNE			
Beaucourt	1		Visited 18, 19 and 20 Battns London Regts. 221 and 288 A.T.C – R.E. Admitted 9 cases for evacuation. Inspected 46 remounts. Having one inspected officer with ophthalmia. Section shelters used for men's billets & also out of bounds by Gas officer.	
"	2		Visited 3 Co. Train. Found new site for Mobile Section at T29.a.82.57P. Proceeded Section leaving 1 NCO and 3 men at Beaucourt on Bottestery Post.	
			D.A.D.V.S visited and inspected 17 horses and 1 mule for evacuation. All sick cases admitted	
T29.a.82.57P	3		Visited Divnl Hqs. 221 and 288 A.T.C. R.E. Sectn Resting. D.A.D.V.S. visited. 3 sick cases admitted	
	4		D.A.D.V.S inspected cases for evacuation. Noal. Visited advanced post and 3 Co. Train	
	5		D.A.D.V.S visited and inspected evacuation cases. Noal. Proceeded on 14 days leave to England	

A6945 Wt. W14422/M1160 350,000 12/16 D. D. & L. Forms/C/2118/14

Army Form C. 2118.

WAR DIARY
or
INTELLIGENCE SUMMARY.
(Erase heading not required.)

1/2ND LONDON MOBILE VETERINARY SECTION
No.
Date June 1918.

Instructions regarding War Diaries and Intelligence Summaries are contained in F. S. Regs., Part II. and the Staff Manual respectively. Title pages will be prepared in manuscript.

Place	Date	Hour	Summary of Events and Information	Remarks and references to Appendices
	JUNE			
T.29.a.82.57.	6		D.O.D.V.S visits Section and Collecting post inspection 8 cases for evacuation. 1 sick case admitted	
"	7		D.Q.3.N and Lieut W"Kae visited Collecting post and Section. 1 case evacuated. 2 horses and 8 others admitted.	
"	8		D.A.D.V.S. inspects 9 cases at Collecting post for evacuation. Sick & lame horses seen. Returns rend'd. 9 sick cases admitted	
"	9		D.A.D.V.S. inspected 8 horses and 1 mule for evacuation. 5 sick animals admitted	
"	10		A.D.V.S. III Corps visits Evacuating post. D.A.D.V.S. and Lieut Collier R.D. visit Section. 4 sick animals admitted.	
"	11		D.A.D.V.S. visits Collecting post and inspects 6 animals for evacuation	

Army Form C. 2118.

WAR DIARY
or
INTELLIGENCE SUMMARY.

(Erase heading not required.)

1/2ND LONDON MOBILE VETERINARY SECTION
No. ....
Date June 1918.

Instructions regarding War Diaries and Intelligence Summaries are contained in F. S. Regs., Part II. and the Staff Manual respectively. Title pages will be prepared in manuscript.

Place	Date	Hour	Summary of Events and Information	Remarks and references to Appendices
T.29.A.82.57.	June 12		D.O.D.V.S. visited Section. 1 pack case admitted.	
	13		Floor sent for horse of 510 H.T. Co. A.S.C. by order wired from D.D.V.S. III Corps. P.M. held on animal by Lieut. McBean. Shrapnel carcase, buried. 5 pack cases admitted.	
	14		D.O.D.V.S. visited collecting post and examined 5 horses and 2 mules for evacuation. 6 pack cases admitted.	
	15		D.O.D.V.S. examined collecting post and Section. Float sent to collect sick cow of 104 Bde R.F.A. Returns rendered.	
	16		D.O.D.V.S. visited Section. A.D.M.S. visited collecting post. 6 pack cases admitted.	
	17		D.O.D.V.S. inspected 8 horses and 4 mules for evacuation. D.O.A.G. visited collecting post. 6 pack cases admitted.	

Army Form C. 2118.

WAR DIARY
or
INTELLIGENCE SUMMARY.
(Erase heading not required.)

1/2ND LONDON MOBILE VETERINARY SECTION
No. ...1...
Date June 23. 1918.

Instructions regarding War Diaries and Intelligence Summaries are contained in F. S. Regs., Part II. and the Staff Manual respectively. Title pages will be prepared in manuscript.

Place	Date	Hour	Summary of Events and Information	Remarks and references to Appendices
SHEET 57.D. T29.A8.2.	JUNE 18		D.A.D.V.S. visits Section and Collecting Post. To inspect Horses and 2 mules for evacuation. O.C. 21 London M.V.S. calls to take over lines for his Section. 2 Animals admitted.	
"	19		Ordr. received to return Mobility on 20th. Bivouac hiring Tel. 21st. D.A.D.V.S. and D.O.D.V.S & J 58 Corps visits. 5 Animals admitted.	
"	20		D.A.D.V.S. visits Collecting Post to inspect animals for evacuation. Collecting Post taken over by 21 London D.V.S.	
BREILLY	21		Section moves to Breilly. Risen from Rest.	
"	22		Rept. return from leave to D.A.D.V.S. American 5th London Fd. Amb. attached. Strength Returns.	
"	23		Visit 3 Co. Heavy Pack animals admitted for evacuation. D.A.D.V.S. visits Section.	

Army Form C. 2118.

1/2ND LONDON MOBILE VETERINARY SECTION
No. ....
Date June 1918

WAR DIARY
or
INTELLIGENCE SUMMARY.
(Erase heading not required.)

Instructions regarding War Diaries and Intelligence Summaries are contained in F. S. Regs., Part II. and the Staff Manual respectively. Title pages will be prepared in manuscript.

Place	Date	Hour	Summary of Events and Information	Remarks and references to Appendices
	JUNE			
BREILLY	24		Inspected the Horse Ambulance Mobile Section for Entrainment. 1 H.D. unit. Stand Colic. A.D.V.S and D.A.D.V.S visited Section. 3 stragglers horses of Section on London over to M.G. Batt. 7 sick cases admitted	
	25		Inspected S.D.A Section D.A.C. D.A.D.V.L. visited and inspected 12 cases for evacuation. 8 sick cases admitted	
	26		Visited and inspected 5th Lon. Field Amb. Officers conference of V.Os at D.A.D.V.S office. 6 sick cases admitted	
	27		Visited 3/lo Lon. Gen. Hosp. showing completion of 4th 5th and 6th London Field Ambs. 1 animal admitted for evacuation	
	28		D.A.D.V.S visited and inspected. 10 horses and 2 mules for evacuation visited S.A.A. pack lines. 4 sick cases admitted	

Army Form C. 2118.

WAR DIARY
or
INTELLIGENCE SUMMARY.
(Erase heading not required.)

1/2ND LONDON MOBILE VETERINARY SECTION
No ....
Date ... June ... 1918.

Instructions regarding War Diaries and Intelligence Summaries are contained in F. S. Regs., Part II. and the Staff Manual respectively. Title pages will be prepared in manuscript.

Place	Date	Hour	Summary of Events and Information	Remarks and references to Appendices
BREILLY	JUNE 29		Judges S.A.A. station for Shoeing Competition. Visited 3 Bde Hqrs. Sent horse to collect horses from III Div Field Amb'y Wpr. a day or two. 2 sick cases admitted.	
	30		Visited lines of 29 to 5th French Bagg. Sample of pus taken from 1 case which made and pus sent to No 5 Vety Hosp. for examination for organisms to buy dis[?]. D.G.V.S. visited and inspected 9 horses 2 miles for exercise. 1 sick animal admitted for treatment.	

H[?] Lieut O.C.
1/2nd London M.V.S.

WAR DIARY
or
INTELLIGENCE SUMMARY.
(Erase heading not required.)

Army Form C. 2118.

1/2nd LONDON MOBILE VETERINARY SECTION
Date 1918

Place	Date	Hour	Summary of Events and Information	Remarks and references to Appendices
BREILLY	JULY 1		Inspected 517th 518th 520th Field Co's R.E. and 1/4th Royal Welch Fusiliers and judged in the monthly competitions of these units. 2 sick cases admitted.	
"	2		Visited and inspected 1/5th London Field Ambulance. 7 sick cases admitted.	
"	3		Visited and inspected No.3 Co. Train. D.A.D.V.S. visited section and inspected animals for evacuation. 9 Horses and 1 Mule evacuated to No 19 V.E.S.	
"	4		Visited 29 Co. 5th French Engrs. Smears taken from 2 cases of suspected Epizootic Lymphangitis. Slides prepared and sent to No 5 Veterinary Hospital for examination. Inspected 141 Bde. H.Q. 1/18th Battn. 1/19th & 1/20th London Regts and 141 Bde. T.M.B. 5 sick cases admitted.	
"	5		Judged condition of animals in H.Q. Signal Co R.E. in monthly competition. 2 sick cases admitted.	

Army Form C. 2118.

WAR DIARY
or
INTELLIGENCE SUMMARY.
(Erase heading not required.)

1/2ND LONDON MOBILE VETERINARY SECTION

Month JULY
Date 1918.

Instructions regarding War Diaries and Intelligence Summaries are contained in F. S. Regs., Part II. and the Staff Manual respectively. Title pages will be prepared in manuscript.

Place	Date	Hour	Summary of Events and Information	Remarks and references to Appendices
	JULY			
BREILLY	6		Visited 29 Co. 5th French Engrs. and Sections left behind of D. and A. Btys. 235 Bde. R.F.A. 4 sick cases admitted	
"	7		Confined to billets by M.O. with P.U.O. Lieut McGree takes on duties of Section. 3 sick cases admitted. 9 horses evacuated to No 19 Y.E.S.	
"	8		7 sick cases admitted to Section	
"	9		3 sick cases admitted to Section.	
"	10		Evacuated morning 7 horses and 6 mules to 19 Y.E.S. and in the afternoon 5 horses and 3 mules. 8 cases admitted	
"	11		5 horses evacuated to 19 Y.E.S. 5 sick cases admitted.	
"	12		Section moves to Montigny. Resumed duties. 4 sick cases admitted.	

Army Form C. 2118.

12ND LONDON MOBILE VETERINARY SECTION
No. ....
Date JULY 1918

WAR DIARY
or
INTELLIGENCE SUMMARY.
(Erase heading not required.)

Instructions regarding War Diaries and Intelligence Summaries are contained in F. S. Regs., Part II. and the Staff Manual respectively. Title pages will be prepared in manuscript.

Place	Date	Hour	Summary of Events and Information	Remarks and references to Appendices
MONTIGNY	JULY 13		Visited and inspected animals of Divnl. H.Q. and H.Q. Signal Co. R.E. 6 sick cases admitted	
"	14		Visited D.A.D.V.S. office and Divnl. H.Q. 1 sick case admitted	
	15		Inspected S.A.A. Section D.A.C. Visited Divnl. H.Q. and Signal Co. R.E. Evacuated 7 horses and 2 mules. Admitted 6 sick cases	
	16		Visited D.A.D.V.S. office. 8 sick cases admitted	
	17		Inspected 239 A.T.Co. R.E., D. Special Co. R.E., and 156 Labour Co. Evacuated 12 horses and 3 mules. Attended Conference of V.Os at D.A.D.V.S. office. Admitted 11 sick cases.	
	18		Evacuated 9 Horses and 1 Mule. Visited S.A.A. Section D.A.C. Admitted 6 cases sick.	

Army Form C. 2118.

1/2ND LONDON MOBILE VETERINARY SECTION
Month July Date 1918

WAR DIARY
or INTELLIGENCE SUMMARY.
(Erase heading not required.)

Instructions regarding War Diaries and Intelligence Summaries are contained in F. S. Regs., Part II. and the Staff Manual respectively. Title pages will be prepared in manuscript.

Place	Date	Hour	Summary of Events and Information	Remarks and references to Appendices
MONTIGNY	JULY 19		Visited Divl. H.Q. Horses and Divl. Signal Co. and Lines of No 3 Section 21st Divn. H.T. Co. 2 sick cases admitted	
"	20		Inspected 517 and 520th Field Cos. R.E. Evacuated 5 Horses and 2 Mules to 9 V.E.S. Admitted 4 sick cases.	
"	21		Inspected 47th Divnl. Train. Admitted 9 sick cases.	
"	22		Visited Lines of 239 A.T., R.E. Unit moved. Inspected 517th and 520th Field Co. R.E. and 1/1st R.W.F. Evacuated 8 Horses and 5 Mules. Admitted 4 cases.	
"	23		D.A.D.V.S. visited Section. Admitted 11 Cases for evacuation.	
"	24		Divnl. Reserves inspected in Action 1 Rejected for Dental Caries. Attended Conference of V.Os at D.A.D.V.S Office. D.A.D.V.S. as O.i. for Corps Asst. Asst. duties of D.A.D.V.S. Admitted 23 sick cases.	

Army Form C. 2118.

WAR DIARY
or
INTELLIGENCE SUMMARY.
(Erase heading not required.)

1/2ND LONDON MOBILE VETERINARY SECTION
Month: JULY
Date: 1918

Place	Date	Hour	Summary of Events and Information	Remarks and references to Appendices
MONTIGNY	JULY 25		Inspected D.D.R. cases at Section. Evacuated 19 horses and 4 mules to No. 7 V.E.S. Admitted 7 sick cases	
"	26		Visited and inspected Head Quarters Signal Co. R.E., 6th London Field Amb. and S.A.A. Section D.A.C. Admitted 6 cases, sick.	
"	27		Evacuated 8 horses and 3 mules to No 7 V.E.S. Returns rendered. 3 sick cases admitted. Visited D.A.D.V.S. office	
"	28		Inspected S.A.A. section of D.A.C. Admitted 4 sick cases	
"	29		Visited 4/1st & 4/2nd London Field Ambs.— judges for monthly competition. Admitted 3 sick cases.	
"	30		Visited 15th Lond Field Amb. Judged in monthly competition. Evacuated 8 horses and 2 mules to No 7 V.E.S. 4 sick cases admitted.	

Army Form C. 2118.

WAR DIARY
or
INTELLIGENCE SUMMARY.
(Erase heading not required.)

1/2ND LONDON MOBILE VETERINARY SECTION
No. JULY
Date 1918.

Instructions regarding War Diaries and Intelligence Summaries are contained in F. S. Regs., Part II. and the Staff Manual respectively. Title pages will be prepared in manuscript.

Place	Date	Hour	Summary of Events and Information	Remarks and references to Appendices
MONTIGNY	JULY 31.		Drove to Ifs and Prone. Signed Co. visited. Attended conference of V.Os. at D.A.D.V.S. office. 21 sick cases admitted.	

J Craig Capt A.V.C.
Cmd 1/2 London M.V.S.

47
WR-36

CONFIDENTIAL

WAR DIARY

OF

1/2 LONDON MOBILE VETERINARY SECTION.

FROM 1.8.18
TO 31.8.18.

1/2ND
LONDON MOBILE
VETERINARY SECTION
Aug 1918

Army Form C. 2118.

WAR DIARY
or
INTELLIGENCE SUMMARY.
(Erase heading not required.)

Instructions regarding War Diaries and Intelligence Summaries are contained in F. S. Regs., Part II. and the Staff Manual respectively. Title pages will be prepared in manuscript.

1/2ND LONDON MOBILE VETERINARY SECTION
No. ....
Date. AUGUST 1918.

Place	Date 1918	Hour	Summary of Events and Information	Remarks and references to Appendices
MONTIGNY	AUG. 1		Inspected S.A.A. Motor D.A.C. Evacuated 15 horses and 6 mules 5 sick cases admitted.	
"	2		Visited 21st Army A.H.T. Co. Six sick cases admitted.	
"	3		Destroyed Bherger of 2nd Life Guards M.G.Corps. for Epizootic Lymphangitis. Three sick cases admitted.	
"	4		Visited S.A.A. Motor D.A.C. Eight sick cases admitted.	
"	5		Visited 47th Field Ambulance. Evacuated 16 horses and 1 mule. Admitted 4 sick cases.	
"	6		A.D.V.S. Corps. Inspected section. Visited 47th Divnl Train. Six sick cases admitted.	

Army Form C. 2118.

WAR DIARY
or
INTELLIGENCE SUMMARY.
(Erase heading not required.)

1/2ND LONDON MOBILE VETERINARY SECTION AUGUST 1918.

Instructions regarding War Diaries and Intelligence Summaries are contained in F. S. Regs., Part II. and the Staff Manual respectively. Title pages will be prepared in manuscript.

Place	Date 1918	Hour	Summary of Events and Information	Remarks and references to Appendices
MONTIGNY.	AUG. 7		Inspected and judged Shoeing Competition in S.A.A. Section D.A.C.	
"	8		Visited "D" Special Coy R.E. and 156 Labour Coy. Attended Conference of V.Os at D.A.D.V.S office. Evacuated 9 horses and 2 mules. Twelve sick cases admitted.	
"	9		Inspected and Examined Sick Lines of S.A.A Section. Ten sick cases admitted.	
"	10		Evacuated 17 horses and 2 mules. D.A.D.V.S visited Section. Six sick cases admitted.	
"	11		Evacuated 1 case by Boat to No 3 V.E.S. Inspected 67 Remounts retaining 1 x D. and 1 Rider not fit for issue. Admitted 27 sick cases.	
"			Evacuated 25 cases to No. 3 V.E.S. Admitted 3 sick cases. Received orders for moving on the 12TH.	

Army Form C. 2118.

WAR DIARY
or
INTELLIGENCE SUMMARY.
(Erase heading not required.)

1/2ND LONDON MOBILE VETERINARY SECTION
August 1918.

Place	Date 1918 August	Hour	Summary of Events and Information	Remarks and references to Appendices
ST GRATIEN.	12		Section Moved to St. Gratien taking over from No.30 M.V.S. 2 Hair cases. Visited No.3 Co. and No.4 Co. Divnl. Train	
"	13		Visited No.2 Co. Divnl. Train. Admitted 7 sick cases. DADY'S wing Section. Received orders for moving on 14th to BONNAY.	
BONNAY.	14		Section moved to BONNAY taking over from 21 London M.V.S. system Advanced Aid Post. Two flesh cases admitted. left by 21 London M.V.S. Evacuated 2 horses and 6 mules.	
"	15		Visited 140 Ind. Bde. xxx xxx 19 Bde. Cavalry Reicheted. Evacuated 15 sick cases. K.E.S. 11 Horses and 3 mules. Admitted 14 sick cases.	
"	16		Visited 142 Ind. Bde. 11 sick cases admitted.	

Army Form C. 2118.

WAR DIARY
or
INTELLIGENCE SUMMARY.
(Erase heading not required.)

Instructions regarding War Diaries and Intelligence Summaries are contained in F. S. Regs., Part II. and the Staff Manual respectively. Title pages will be prepared in manuscript.

1/2nd LONDON MOBILE VETERINARY SECTION
Date ..August.. 1918.

Place	Date 1918	Hour	Summary of Events and Information	Remarks and references to Appendices
	August			
BONNAY	17		Visited 518 Field Co R.E. Evacuated 12 horses to 1st Aust. V.E.S. 17 sick cases admitted	
"	18		Evacuated 17 horses to V.E.S. failed to trace unit 253 Tunnelling Co. R.E. Map reference inaccurate. 18 sick cases admitted	
"	19		Evacuated 17 horses and 2 mules to V.E.S. Visited 253 Tun. Co. R.E. Admitted 9 sick cases.	
"	20		Evacuated 5 horses and 4 mules to V.E.S. Admitted 15 sick cases	
"	21		Evacuated 8 horses and 5 mules to V.E.S. Visited 518 Field Co. R.E. Attended Conference of V.Os at D.A.D.V.S. office. 14 sick cases admitted. Selected site for Advanced Aid Post at Map 62D. J.22.a.2.8.	

Army Form C. 2118.

1/2ND LONDON MOBILE VETERINARY SECTION
No............ Date AUGUST 1918

WAR DIARY
or
INTELLIGENCE SUMMARY.
(Erase heading not required.)

Instructions regarding War Diaries and Intelligence Summaries are contained in F. S. Regs., Part II. and the Staff Manual respectively. Title pages will be prepared in manuscript.

Place	Date	Hour	Summary of Events and Information	Remarks and references to Appendices
	Aug.			
BONNAY.	22		Established Advanced Aid Post at T.22.A.2.8. Map 62D. Evacuated 10 horses and 3 mules to 1 Aust V.E.S. Admitted 15 sick cases.	
"	23		Evacuated 12 horses and 2 mules. Visited Aid Post. Admitted 33 sick cases	
"	24		Visited Aid Post. Evacuated 29 horses and 2 mules to 1 Australian V.E.S. Admitted 14 sick cases	
"	25		Visited 422nd and 512th London Rgts. Evacuated 10 horses and 4 mules to 1 Aust V.E.S. Admitted 11 sick cases. Twelve sick cases admitted	
"	26		Evacuated 8 horses and 4 mules to 1 Aust V.E.S. Orders received for Section to move to Morcourt	
Morcourt	27		Evacuated 8 horses and 2 mules. Aid Post withdrawn. Section moved to Morcourt. 5 sick cases admitted and evacuated to 1st Aust V.E.S.	

Army Form C. 2118.

1/2ND LONDON MOBILE VETERINARY SECTION
No. AUGUST
Date 1918.

WAR DIARY
or
INTELLIGENCE SUMMARY.
(Erase heading not required.)

Place	Date 1918	Hour	Summary of Events and Information	Remarks and references to Appendices
MERICOURT	Aug. 28		Visited 141 Inf. Bde. Attended conference of V.Os at D.A.D.V.S. office. Three sick cases admitted.	
MÉAULTE	29		Orders received for section to move to MÉAULTE with advanced Adv. Post at Mametz. Evacuated 3 sick cases to No 3. V.E.S. Section moved to MÉAULTE. Advanced Aid Post established at F.4.C.5.4. Map 62D.	
"	30		Visited 22nd and 23rd Battns London Regt. Admitted 18 sick cases. Received orders for move to F.4.C.	
MAP 62.D. F.4.C.	31		Evacuated 8 horses and 1 mule to No 3. V.E.S. Section moved to F.4.C.	

J. Craig Capt A.V.C. T.F.
O.C. 1/2 London M.V.S.

41

CONFIDENTIAL

WL 38

CONFIDENTIAL

WAR DIARY

of

1/2 London Mobile Veterinary Section.

From 1-9-18   To 30-9-18.

Army Form C. 2118.

WAR DIARY
or
INTELLIGENCE SUMMARY.
(Erase heading not required.)

1/2ND LONDON MOBILE VETERINARY SECTION
No. ....
Date SEPT. 1918

Instructions regarding War Diaries and Intelligence Summaries are contained in F. S. Regs., Part II. and the Staff Manual respectively. Title pages will be prepared in manuscript.

Place	Date 1918	Hour	Summary of Events and Information	Remarks and references to Appendices
MAMETZ.	SEPT 1		Evacuated 8 horses and 3 mules to No. 3 V.E.S. Dernancourt. Six horses and one mule admitted	
"	2		D.A.D.V.S visited and inspected horses for evacuation. 6 horses and 4 mules evacuated. Six horses and 4 mules admitted.	
"	3		Evacuated 6 horses and 1 mule. Admitted 2 horses and 1 mule.	
"	4		Attended Conference at D.A.D.V.S. office of V.Os of the Division. Admitted 3 horses for evacuation.	
Hardicourt	5		Visited 141 Inf. Bde. Found site near Hardicourt for Section. Section moved to Hardicourt. Evacuated 5 horses and 1 mule. Admitted 4 horses. Visited 19th and 20th Battns London Regt.	
"	6		Visited D.A.D.V.S at Maurepas. Admitted 2 horses for evacuation.	

Army Form C. 2118.

1/2ND LONDON MOBILE VETERINARY SECTION
Date SEPT 1918

WAR DIARY
or
INTELLIGENCE SUMMARY.
(Erase heading not required.)

Instructions regarding War Diaries and Intelligence Summaries are contained in F. S. Regs., Part II. and the Staff Manual respectively. Title pages will be prepared in manuscript.

Place	Date 1918	Hour	Summary of Events and Information	Remarks and references to Appendices
	SEPT			
CORBIE	7		Section moved to CORBIE. Casualties and cases for treatment evacuated to horses to V.F.S.	
	8		Visited 3 Co A.S.C. and 20th Bath London Regt.	
HEILLY	9		Section moved to HEILLY to entrain	
	10		Section detrained at CHOCQUES and moved to CALONNE RICQUART	
	11		Visited D.A.D.V.S. and 1/9th London Regt.	
	12		Visited Field Cashier. Drew £10.0.0 and issued 1 Subs account for ordnance.	
	13		Visited 18th 19th 20th London Regts and 141 Bde H.Q. Casualties and sick horses and mules for evacuation. Visited D.A.D.V.S.	

Army Form C. 2118.

1/2ND LONDON MOBILE VETERINARY SECTION
No. SEPT
Date 1918

WAR DIARY
or INTELLIGENCE SUMMARY.
(Erase heading not required.)

Instructions regarding War Diaries and Intelligence Summaries are contained in F. S. Regs., Part II. and the Staff Manual respectively. Title pages will be prepared in manuscript.

Place	Date 1918	Hour	Summary of Events and Information	Remarks and references to Appendices
LAPUGNOY	SEPT. 14		Section moved to LAPUGNOY. Inspected Divisional Remounts. 5 Riders 86 L.D. & 29 Mules. Admitted 2 Cases for evacuation.	
"	15		Visited 5th London Field Amb. 7 horses admitted for evacuation	
"	16		Visited 517, 518, and 520 Field Coys. R.E. and 6 R.E. Head Qrs. Sent 1 case of Ulcer Lyhhatica from 518 Field Co. R.E. To Mobile Section for Evacuation. 8 cases admitted for evacuation.	
"	17		Evacuated 11 horses and 1 mule. To No.13 V.E.S. 5 cases admitted	
"	18		Visited 5th London Field Amb. Admitted 6 horses and 3 mules	
"	19		Evacuated 10 horses and 6 mules To No.13 V.E.S. D.A.D.V.S. A.D.V.S. visit Section. 2 cases admitted. 47th Divl. Administration Instructions No.12 dated Sept 18th 1918 received.	

Army Form C. 2118.

WAR DIARY
or
INTELLIGENCE SUMMARY.

(Erase heading not required.)

1/2ND LONDON MOBILE VETERINARY SECTION
No. ....
Date SEPT 1918

Instructions regarding War Diaries and Intelligence Summaries are contained in F. S. Regs., Part II. and the Staff Manual respectively. Title pages will be prepared in manuscript.

Place	Date 1918	Hour	Summary of Events and Information	Remarks and references to Appendices
LAPUGNOY	SEPT 20		ADVS XIII Corps and D.D.V.S. V Army visit and inspect Section. 1 Case admitted for evacuation	
"	21		D.A.D.V.S. visits Section. Evacuated 4 Animals to V.E.S. Admitted 3 sick cases.	
"	22		Section in readiness to entrain at 1 hours notice. Evacuated 2 cases to V.E.S. Admitted one case.	
"	23		Visited 19th and 20th London Regts and 1/1st Royal Welsh Fusiliers. Move postponed.	
"	24		Visited R.E. lines found Units moved. Visited BRIAS to arrange for Billets for 56 Horses of Division.	
"	25		Evacuated 4 horses to V.E.S. Visited 3 Co. A.S.C.	

WAR DIARY
or
INTELLIGENCE SUMMARY.

(Erase heading not required.)

Army Form C. 2118.

T/2ND LONDON MOBILE VETERINARY SECTION
SEPT. 1918.

Place	Date 1918 SEPT.	Hour	Summary of Events and Information	Remarks and references to Appendices
LAPUGNOY	26		Attended Conference of V.Os at D.A.D.V.S. office. Returns rendered. Orders received for Section to move with 141 Bde Group to HERNICOURT.	
HERNICOURT	27		Section moved to HERNICOURT. Inspected by D.O.B. en route. Evacuated 2 cases to No 13 V.E.S. Admitted one case for evacuation.	
	28		Visited D.A.D.V.S. office at HAUTCLOCQUE. 2 cases admitted for evacuation.	
	29.		Visited 3 Co. A.S.C. and 141 Bde Headqtrs. 2 cases admitted for evacuation.	
	30		Evacuated 4 horses to No. 2 Collecting Post at Pol.	

J. Craig Cap' AVC T.F.

To:
D.A.D.V.S. 29
47th Divn

Herewith please receive War Diary for month ending October 31st 1918.

1/2ND LONDON MOBILE VETERINARY SECTION
No. M 342
Date 1-11-18

J Craig Capt AVC
Omdg 1/2 London M.V.S.

CONFIDENTIAL

WAR DIARY.

of
1/2 London Mobile Veterinary Section

From October 1st, 1918
To October 31st 1918.

Army Form C. 2118.

WAR DIARY
or
INTELLIGENCE SUMMARY.
(Erase heading not required.)

1/2ND LONDON MOBILE VETERINARY SECTION
Date OCTBR. 1918.

Instructions regarding War Diaries and Intelligence Summaries are contained in F. S. Regs., Part II. and the Staff Manual respectively. Title pages will be prepared in manuscript.

Place	Date 1918	Hour	Summary of Events and Information	Remarks and references to Appendices
NEDON	OCT. 1		Section moved from HERNICOURT to NEDON.	
LESTRUM	2		Section moved from NEDON to LESTRUM.	
"	3		Moved to take over Advanced collecting post from 2/1 West Riding M.V.S. One case admitted from N.R. Hy. Arty. D.A.D.V.S. visits section.	
"	4		Orders received to prepare for move. Two Horse cases admitted.	
PONT DU HEM	5		Moved Half of Section to Pont du Hem. Evacuates 3 cases to V.E.S. including 1 Horse case.	
"	6		Rear half of section arrives at Pont du Hem. D.A.D.V.S. visits section. Visited No. 3 Co A.S.C. 6 pack cases admitted.	

Army Form C. 2118.

1/2ND LONDON MOBILE VETERINARY SECTION
Date OCTOBER 1918

WAR DIARY
or
INTELLIGENCE SUMMARY.
(Erase heading not required.)

Instructions regarding War Diaries and Intelligence Summaries are contained in F. S. Regs., Part II. and the Staff Manual respectively. Title pages will be prepared in manuscript.

Place	Date 1918 Oct.	Hour	Summary of Events and Information	Remarks and references to Appendices
PONT DU HEM	7		Inspected 141 Bde H.Q., 1/18 Battn, 1/19th and 1/20th Battns and reported on condition of horse standing and one case with lacerated wound to M.V.S. for evacuation. Three cases admitted to section.	
"	8		Visited 1/22nd, 1/23rd and 1/24th Battns and reported on condition of horse lines to B.H.Q. 6 pick cases admitted.	
"	9		Evacuated 13 horses and 1 mule to No 11 V.E.S. Inspected stabling and horses of 4th London Field Ambulance. 12 pick cases admitted.	
"	10		Evacuated 10 horses and 1 mule. Visited 1/22nd, 1/23rd and 1/24th Battns. D.A.D.V.S. visits section. 9 cases admitted for evacuation.	
"	11		Visited 141 I.F. Bde. A D.V.S. XI Corps visits section. 8 horses admitted for evacuation.	

Army Form C. 2118.

WAR DIARY
or
INTELLIGENCE SUMMARY.
(Erase heading not required.)

Instructions regarding War Diaries and Intelligence Summaries are contained in F. S. Regs., Part II. and the Staff Manual respectively. Title pages will be prepared in manuscript.

1/2ND LONDON MOBILE VETERINARY SECTION
Mo. OCTOBER
Date 1918

Place	Date 1918	Hour	Summary of Events and Information	Remarks and references to Appendices
PONT DU HEM	OCT 12		Inspected 1/4th London Field Ambulance and No 2 Co. Div. Train. Evacuated 12 horses and 2 mules to No 11 V.E.S. 1 mule admitted	
"	13		Evacuated one Heat Case to No. 11 V.E.S. Admitted 2 sick cases.	
"	14		Visited 1/22nd and 1/23rd London Regts. Evacuated 4 horses to V.E.S. Admitted 4 horses	
"	15		Evacuated one Heat Case to No 11 V.E.S. Visited 1/24th London Regt.	
"	16		Evacuated 4 horses and 1 mule to V.E.S. Visited Headquarters of V.O. at D.A.D.V.S. office. 6 horses and 3 mules admitted to section.	
"	17		Visited 57th Divl M.V.S. to arrange for this taking over lines and linkage of this Section. Billeting party sent on to MAZINGHEM. Evacuated 5 horses and 2 mules to V.E.S. including one Heat Case.	

A6945 Wt. W14422/M1160 350,000 12/16 D. D. & L. Forms/C./2118/14.

Army Form C. 2118.

WAR DIARY
or
INTELLIGENCE SUMMARY.
(Erase heading not required.)

1/2ND LONDON MOBILE VETERINARY SECTION
Month OCTOBER
Date 1918.

Instructions regarding War Diaries and Intelligence Summaries are contained in F. S. Regs., Part II. and the Staff Manual respectively. Title pages will be prepared in manuscript.

Place	Date 1918	Hour	Summary of Events and Information	Remarks and references to Appendices
MAZINGHEM	OCT 18		Section moved to MAZINGHEM. 57th Divn. M.V.S. refused to take over horses on postage	
"	19		Visited D.A.D.V.S. to find location of V.F.S.	
"	20		D.A.D.V.S. visits Section. One case admitted for evacuation	
"	21		Visited 141 Inf. Bde. H.Q., 1/19th and 1/20th London Regts. Admitted 2 cases	
"	22		Visited 1/18th London Regt and 47th M.G. Battn. 9 horses and 2 mules admitted	
"	23		Visited 4th Royal Welsh Fusiliers. Inspected Remounts for the Division retaining 2 L.Do unfit for issue. Five sick cases admitted	
"	24		Evacuated 17 cases by road to No 23 Veterinary Hospl. Attended Conference of V.Os. 2 Butcher cases sold to M.DELBAR LILLERS. Arrived 850 Hs. Admitted 8 cases	

Army Form C. 2118.

WAR DIARY
or
INTELLIGENCE SUMMARY.
(Erase heading not required.)

1/2ND LONDON MOBILE VETERINARY SECTION
Mo. 1918
Date. OCTOBER.

Place	Date 1918	Hour	Summary of Events and Information	Remarks and references to Appendices
ESTAIRES.	OCT. 25		Section moved to ESTAIRES. One carcase left at Praying Farm for collection by M. DELBAR. LILLERS.	
LOMME	26		Section moved to LOMME. One case admitted for evacuation.	
"	27		Visited 3 Co. ASC. Billeting party sent to FIVES. Visited DADVS. office for location of V.E.S. Attended Conference.	
FIVES- LILLE	28		March through LILLE – 5th Army Official entrance. Moved section to FIVES- LILLE.	
"	29		Visited 1/5th London Field Ambulance. No 3 Co. Han and D.A.D.V.S. office. Horse sent to collect case left behind by D/235 Bde. Case Evacuated back cases to V.E.S. Sent direct to V.E.S.	

Army Form C. 2118.

1/2ND LONDON MOBILE VETERINARY SECTION
No. 1918
Date OCTOBER

WAR DIARY
or
INTELLIGENCE SUMMARY.
(Erase heading not required.)

Instructions regarding War Diaries and Intelligence Summaries are contained in F. S. Regs., Part II. and the Staff Manual respectively. Title pages will be prepared in manuscript.

Place	Date 1918	Hour	Summary of Events and Information	Remarks and references to Appendices
FIVES-LILLE	OCT. 30		Visited 57th Divl M.V.S. to arrange to take over on Friday 1st November.	
			One sick case admitted	
	31		D.A.D.V.S. visited Section. Advanced party sent to take over from 57d Divl. M.V.S. One case evacuated.	
			J Craig Cap'n A.V.C. T.F.	

Army Form C. 2118.

WAR DIARY
or
INTELLIGENCE SUMMARY.
(Erase heading not required.)

1/2ND LONDON MOBILE VETERINARY SECTION
No.....................
Date.. 1/12/18

Instructions regarding War Diaries and Intelligence Summaries are contained in F. S. Regs., Part II. and the Staff Manual respectively. Title pages will be prepared in manuscript.

Place	Date 1918	Hour	Summary of Events and Information	Remarks and references to Appendices
WILLEMS	Nov 1		Section moved to WILLEMS from FIVES-LILLE. Visited 1st Lndn Field Ambulance and inspected stabling. 3 sick cases admitted.	
	2		Returns rendered. 5 sick cases admitted 1 "horse" for execution	
	3		Visited 1/33rd Lndn Regt.	
			" 1/23rd Lndn Regt. 17 sick cases admitted for execution	
	4		Visited 1/20th Lndn Regt and 142-B & H.Q. 1/24 Ln. Train. 17 sick cases admitted. Evacuated to 1st V.E.S. 19 horses and 5 mules	
	5		Visited 1/5th, 1/7th and 1/21st Lndn Regt. 5 sick cases admitted. Evacuated to 1st V.E.S. 13 horses and 3 mules	
	6		I.R. returned to 47 S.9 H. attached to 47 S.Div 4 sick cases admitted	

John MacBride
Capt A.V.C.

Army Form C. 2118.

WAR DIARY
or
INTELLIGENCE SUMMARY.
(Erase heading not required.)

1/2ND LONDON MOBILE VETERINARY SECTION

Place	Date	Hour	Summary of Events and Information	Remarks and references to Appendices
WILLEMS	1915 Nov. 7		Visited H.Q. 1. & 3. F.A., 1 sick case admitted, and evacuated 8 horses and 1 Mule to No. 11 V.E.S.	
	8		Visited R.H.Q. to Train and the 2nd London Regt. Visited Field bookers and evacuated 8 horses and 1 Mule to No. 11 V.E.S.	
	9		Returns rendered and inspected 1/4th London Regt and 1/2nd London Regt.	
	10		Visited Auguennes after Signal Sgts at Blandain. Evacuated 5 horses and 4 Mules.	
	11		Section moved to Auguennes. 1 sick horse admitted.	
	12		Visited the D.A.D.V.S. and 1/17th London Regt. 1 sick Horse admitted.	
	13		Visited 1/17 London Regt Lines and destroyed 1 H.D. Horse, 2 sick cases admitted.	

John MacBride
Capt. A.V.C.

Army Form C. 2118.

WAR DIARY
or
INTELLIGENCE SUMMARY.
(Erase heading not required.)

Instructions regarding War Diaries and Intelligence Summaries are contained in F. S. Regs., Part II. and the Staff Manual respectively. Title pages will be prepared in manuscript.

1/2ND LONDON MOBILE VETERINARY SECTION
No.............
Date 1/12/18

Place	Date	Hour	Summary of Events and Information	Remarks and references to Appendices
FROYENNES	1918 Nov. 14		Conference at A.D.V.S. office, 4 cases admitted	
	15		Inspected and passed 22 Remounts, 2 cases admitted and ordered reinoculated to hairs and 1 horse to No 3 V.E.J.	
	16		Returns rendered. Section moved to Lothery, evacuated 1 horse and 1 horse to No 3 V.E.J.	
CHERENG	17		Visited O.L. and L.L. and No 2 L.C. Train	
	18		Returns rendered	
	19		Visited 1/4th R.W.F. and inspected stables	
	20		Visited 1/19th and 1/21st London Regts at Willems, 2 cases admitted	

John Brackbrill
Capt. A.V.C.

Army Form C. 2118.

1/2ND LONDON MOBILE VETERINARY SECTION
Date 1/12/18

WAR DIARY
or
INTELLIGENCE SUMMARY.
(Erase heading not required.)

Place	Date	Hour	Summary of Events and Information	Remarks and references to Appendices
CHERENG	1918 Nov 21		Visited 1/20 London Regt, conference at D.A.D.V.S. also evacuated 20 horses to 11 C.C.S.	
	22		Returns rendered, visited field cashier	
	23		Returns received, Inspected 1/4 London Field Ambulance standing stables 1/5 London Field Ambulance stables	
	24		Evacuated 2 horses and 2 mules and prepared to move section	
	25		Visited Supply with D.A.D.V.S. and selected billets for section	
	26		Inspected 4/7 and 4/21 London Regts, on March, evacuated 4 horses and 1 mule	
	27		Moved from Cohung to Habrudin	

John MacBrille
Capt A.V.C.

Army Form C. 2118.

1/2ND LONDON MOBILE VETERINARY SECTION
No.
Date 1/3/18

WAR DIARY
or
INTELLIGENCE SUMMARY.
(Erase heading not required.)

Instructions regarding War Diaries and Intelligence Summaries are contained in F. S. Regs., Part II. and the Staff Manual respectively. Title pages will be prepared in manuscript.

Place	Date	Hour	Summary of Events and Information	Remarks and references to Appendices
	1918 Nov 28		Moved from Hebuterne to Lafuguy	
	29		Moved from Lafuguy to Lagny. Visited 1/16th London Regt	
	30		Return rendered. D.A.D.V.S. visited Section	

John MacBryde
Lt AVC

Army Form C. 2118.

1/2ND LONDON MOBILE VETERINARY SECTION
1918 DECEMBER

WAR DIARY
or
INTELLIGENCE SUMMARY.
(Erase heading not required.)

Place	Date 1918	Hour	Summary of Events and Information	Remarks and references to Appendices
MAP. 5.A. FERFAY	DEC. 1		Visited 20th Battn London Regt. and D.a.D.V.D. Three sick cases admitted for evacuation	
"	2		Visited 1/15th Batt. London Regt. and AMETTES To collect animals left by unknown unit (Artillery) with an inhabitant. One case admitted to section	
"	3		Visited 4th Infantry Bde. and 15th London Field Amb. Five sick cases admitted for evacuation	
"	4		Evacuation to No. 11. V.E.S. 8 horses and 2 mules Visited 1/21st Battn London Regt. and 1/15th London Regt. One sick case admitted	
"	5		Visited Conference of V.Os at D.A.D.V.S. office. Five cases admitted for evacuation	

Army Form C. 2118.

WAR DIARY
—or—
INTELLIGENCE SUMMARY.
(Erase heading not required.)

Instructions regarding War Diaries and Intelligence Summaries are contained in F. S. Regs., Part II. and the Staff Manual respectively. Title pages will be prepared in manuscript.

1/2ND LONDON MOBILE VETERINARY SECTION
No. 1918
Date DEC.

Place	Date 1918	Hour	Summary of Events and Information	Remarks and references to Appendices
MAP 44B E.7.c.27	DEC. 6		Section moved to site MAP 44B E.7.c.27. Two pack mules admitted	
"	7		Evacuated 4 horses and 2 mules to No 11 V.E.S. Weekly returns rendered. D.A.D.V.S. visited.	
"	8		Visited D.D.V.S office and 4/th Div Train. Two horses and one mule admitted for evacuation.	
"	9		Visited D.A.D.V.S office and Field Cashier. Admitted two sick cases.	
"	10		Evacuated 4 horses and 1 mule to No 11 V.E.S. Visited 6th London Field Amb., 24th Battn. London Regt. H.Q. 142 Inf. Bde and 9/03 Lws to Co Disl Train. Eight cases admitted for evacuation	

Army Form C. 2118.

WAR DIARY
or
INTELLIGENCE SUMMARY.
(Erase heading not required.)

Instructions regarding War Diaries and Intelligence Summaries are contained in F. S. Regs. Part II. and the Staff Manual respectively. Title pages will be prepared in manuscript.

1/2ND LONDON MOBILE VETERINARY SECTION
No. 19
Date DECEMBER 1918

Place	Date 1918	Hour	Summary of Events and Information	Remarks and references to Appendices
MAP 44B E7C 2.7.	DEC. 11		Evacuated eight cases to No. 11 V.E.S. D.A.D.V.S. visited Section	
"	12		A.D.V.S. visited and inspected Section. One case admitted for evacuation.	
"	13		D.A.D.V.S. visited Section	
"	14		Evacuated eight case to V.E.S. Visited both A.Tk. and D.A.D.V.S. Ten cases admitted to Section.	
"	15		D.A.D.V.S. visited Section. Evacuated 8 horses and 1 mule to V.E.S.	
"	16		Ran in 400 trees to Field Cashier at Div. H.Q. for Butcher Bros. 12 sick cases admitted to Section. Thirteen cases evacuated to V.E.S.	

Army Form C. 2118.

WAR DIARY
or
INTELLIGENCE SUMMARY.
(Erase heading not required.)

1/2ND LONDON MOBILE VETERINARY SECTION
No. ....
Date DECEMBER 1918

Instructions regarding War Diaries and Intelligence Summaries are contained in F. S. Regs., Part II. and the Staff Manual respectively. Title pages will be prepared in manuscript.

Place	Date 1918	Hour	Summary of Events and Information	Remarks and references to Appendices
MAP. 44B E.7.C.2.7.	DEC. 17		Admitted 3 cases for evacuation. D.A.D.V.S. visited section	
"	18		Visited 142nd Bde. H.Qrs. 1/1st London Field Amb. and 1/24th London Regt.	
"	19		Attended Conference of V.Os. at D.A.D.V.S. Office. Admitted 3 mules three cases for evacuation	
"	20		Evacuated 5 horses and 1 mule to V.E.S. Visited D.A.D.V.S. office. Three sick cases admitted	
"	21		Inspected H.Qrs. 142 Inf. Bde. 1/22nd, 1/23rd and 1/24th London Regt. Visited D.A.D.V.S. Office. Admitted 5 cases for evacuation	
"	22		Evacuated 4 horses and 1 mule sick cases and 3 horses and 1 mule cast by D.D.R. to V.E.S.	

Army Form C. 2118.

WAR DIARY
or
INTELLIGENCE SUMMARY.
(Erase heading not required.)

1/2ND LONDON MOBILE VETERINARY SECTION
Month 1918 DECEMBER

Instructions regarding War Diaries and Intelligence Summaries are contained in F. S. Regs., Part II. and the Staff Manual respectively. Title pages will be prepared in manuscript.

Place	Date 1918	Hour	Summary of Events and Information	Remarks and references to Appendices
MAP. 44.B. E.7.c.2.7.	DEC. 23		Visited Divl Head Quarters and D.A.D.V.S. office. Eight cases admitted for evacuation	
"	24		Evacuated 7 Horses and 1 mule to V.E.S. Inspected 141 Inf Bde H.26. 1/18st, 1/19th, and 1/20th Battns London Regts. One sick case admitted	
"	25		Capt MacBride and Lt McCrea visited Section. Section Dinner	
"	26		Attended Conference of V.Os. at D.A.D.V.S. office. Visited Divisional H.Qtrs Transport. 21 cases admitted for evacuation.	
"	27		Evacuated 24 Horses and 1 mule to V.E.S. Visited D.A.D.V.S office. 3 sick cases admitted	
"	28		Inspected and judged condition of animals of 1/4th 1/5th and 1/6th London Field Ambulances in monthly competition. Two cases admitted	

Army Form C. 2118.

WAR DIARY
or
INTELLIGENCE SUMMARY.
(Erase heading not required.)

1/2ND LONDON MOBILE VETERINARY SECTION
No. 19
Date DECEMBER 1918

Place	Date 1918.	Hour	Summary of Events and Information	Remarks and references to Appendices
MAP. H.L.B. E7.c.2.7	DEC. 29.		Visit Div. H.Qrs. Transport lines, and D.A.D.V.D. office	
"	30		Inspected animals of Divisional train and shared in Inspection of section of animals. Visited 520 Held Coy R.E. Admitted 3 Oxen for evacuation	
"	31		Evacuated 27 horses and 6 mules to V.E.S. 32 animals admitted for evacuation. Visited 142 Bde H.Qrs. '142 [Sendi?] Club' and Visitors Flea Club.	

J Craig Bur RAVC
O.C. 1/2 London M.V.S.

Army Form C. 2118.

WAR DIARY
or
INTELLIGENCE SUMMARY.

(Erase heading not required.)

1/2ND LONDON MOBILE VETERINARY SECTION
No. JANUARY
Date 1919.

Vol 42

Place	Date 1919	Hour	Summary of Events and Information	Remarks and references to Appendices
MAP 44B E.7.C.2.7.	JAN 1		Visited 520 Field Co. R.E. and evacuated 8 cases to Mobile Section for evacuation. 2 sick cases admitted to Section.	
"	2		Attended Conference of V.Os. at D.A.D.V.S. office.	
"	3		Visited A.D.V.S. office and Field Cashier XI Corps. Evacuated 19 horses and 2 mules to No. 11. V.E.S. Visited H.Q. horses. 17 Animals admitted.	
"	4		Attended on the Veterinary Board for classification of the animals of the Division.	
"	5		Attended Veterinary Board.	
"	6		Attended Veterinary Board.	
"	7		Attended Veterinary Board. One mule admitted for evacuation	

Army Form C. 2118.

WAR DIARY
or
INTELLIGENCE SUMMARY.
(Erase heading not required.)

1/2ND LONDON MOBILE VETERINARY SECTION
JANUARY 1919

Instructions regarding War Diaries and Intelligence Summaries are contained in F. S. Regs., Part II. and the Staff Manual respectively. Title pages will be prepared in manuscript.

Place	Date 1919	Hour	Summary of Events and Information	Remarks and references to Appendices
MAP 44B F.7.C.2.7	JAN 8		Attended on Veterinary Board. One case admitted for evacuation	
"	9		Attended on Veterinary Board. Admitted 42 animals for evacuation	
"	10		Attended on Veterinary Board. Evacuated 42 horses and 2 mules to No 11 V.E.S.	
"	11		Attended on Veterinary Board.	
"	12		Attended on Veterinary Board	
"	13		Attended on Veterinary Board. One stray mule admitted	
"	14		Attended on Veterinary Board.	
"	15		Attended on Veterinary Board.	

Army Form C. 2118.

WAR DIARY
or
INTELLIGENCE SUMMARY.
(Erase heading not required.)

1/2ND LONDON MOBILE VETERINARY SECTION
Month JANUARY
Date 1919

Place	Date 1919 JAN.	Hour	Summary of Events and Information	Remarks and references to Appendices
MAP 44B E7.C27	16		Attended on Veterinary Board. Admitted 47 cases for evacuation. Evacuated 44 horses and 3 mules to M.V.E.S.	
"	17		Attended on Veterinary Board. Admitted 1 sick case and 1 stray mule.	
"	18		Attended on Veterinary Board.	
"	19		Attended on Veterinary Board.	
"	20		Attended on Veterinary Board. One sick case admitted.	
"	21		Attended on Veterinary Board.	
"	22		Attended on Veterinary Board.	
"	23		Attended on Veterinary Board. Eight horses and one mule admitted.	

Army Form C. 2118.

WAR DIARY
or
INTELLIGENCE SUMMARY.
(Erase heading not required.)

1/2ND LONDON MOBILE VETERINARY SECTION
No.
Date JANUARY 1919

Instructions regarding War Diaries and Intelligence Summaries are contained in F. S. Regs., Part II. and the Staff Manual respectively. Title pages will be prepared in manuscript.

Place	Date	Hour	Summary of Events and Information	Remarks and references to Appendices
MAP. 44B. E.7.C.2.7.	1919 JAN. 24		Attended on Veterinary Board. Evacuated 10 horses and 2 mules to V.E.S. Admitted one sick case	
"	25		Attended on Veterinary Board	
"	26		Admitted 3 horses and 3 mules for evacuation. D.A.D.V.S. visited	
"	27		Attended Veterinary Board	
"	28		Visited Field Bakery XI Corps.	
"	29		Evacuated 4 horses and 3 mules to V.E.S.	
"	30		Attended Conference of V.Os. at D.A.D.V.S. office. Admitted 8 horses and 2 mules for evacuation.	

Army Form C. 2118.

WAR DIARY
or
INTELLIGENCE SUMMARY.
(Erase heading not required.)

1/2ND LONDON MOBILE VETERINARY SECTION
No. ....
JANUARY
Date .... 1919 ....

Place	Date 1919	Hour	Summary of Events and Information	Remarks and references to Appendices
MAP 44B E.7.C.27.	JAN. 31.		D.A.D.V. visits Section. Evacuated 29 horses and 2 mules to V.E.S. Admitted 22 cases.	

J Craig Capt R.A.V.C.
O/md 1/2 London M.V.S

WAR DIARY
or
INTELLIGENCE SUMMARY.
(Erase heading not required.)

Instructions regarding War Diaries and Intelligence Summaries are contained in F. S. Regs., Part II. and the Staff Manual respectively. Title pages will be prepared in manuscript.

Place	Date 1919	Hour	Summary of Events and Information
LABEUVRIERE	FEB 1		Visited D.A.C. Office routine.
"	2		Section Routine.
"	3		Visited DADVS office and Field Butcher DADVS and DDDR visit section
"	4		Visited 1/4 Royal Welch Fus. pending on Sin cases to Mobile Section for evacuation.
"	5		Evacuated 9 horses and 1 mule to No 11 V.E.S. Animals admitted 10.
"	6		Attended Conference at DADVS office. Animals admitted 15.
"	7		Visited Royal Welsh Fus. Evacuated 9 horses and 6 mules. 1 case admitted

WAR DIARY or INTELLIGENCE SUMMARY.

(Erase heading not required.)

Army Form

Instructions regarding War Diaries and Intelligence Summaries are contained in F. S. Regs., Part II. and the Staff Manual respectively. Title pages will be prepared in manuscript.

Place	Date 1919	Hour	Summary of Events and Information	Remarks and references to Appendices
LABOUVRIERE	FEB 8		D.A.D.V.S. and D.A.D.R. visited Section. Office Routine. Returns rendered.	
"	9		Section Routine. Visited 1/21 Royal Welch Fus.	
"	10		Visited 1/22 London Regt. and inspected 7 milch cows at farm in LA REVEILLON. — Four animals found suffering from Variola Vaccinia. Revisited farm at LA REVEILLON. Three animals admitted to Section.	
"	11		Retested one A.D.I.M.G. Battn. — Mallein. and O.C. 1/5th London Field Ambce.	
"	12		Test-Mallein. 101 L.D. of M.G. Battn. Negative. Malleined 96 horses at Section of 142 Inf. Bde.	
"	13		Inspected 1/22nd 1/23rd & 1/24th London Regts. and 142 Inf. Bde. H.Q. Attended Conference at D.D.V.S. Office. Animals admitted Feb 13.	

Army Form C. 2118.

WAR DIARY
or
INTELLIGENCE SUMMARY.
(Erase heading not required.)

Instructions regarding War Diaries and Intelligence Summaries are contained in F. S. Regs., Part II. and the Staff Manual respectively. Title pages will be prepared in manuscript.

Place	Date 1919	Hour	Summary of Events and Information	Remarks and references to Appendices
LA BEUVRIERE	FEB 14		Evacuated 12 Horses and 2 Mules to 9.11 V.E.S. Section Routine	
"	15		Animals admitted 8 horses and 2 mules. Evacuated 8 horses and 1 mule to 9.11 V.E.S. Office Routine – Returns rendered.	
"	16		Section Routine	
"	17		Visited Corps Field Bakeries Paying in 350 frs. money obtained for Butcher cask	
"	18		Arranged with Mon MOCQ Bruay to buy 2 "D" Cases or 4/5 francs each. Instructions received to take charge of 2 1% at PREVENT	
"	19		Visited D.H.Q and 141 Inf Bde. Selected 20 horses and 10 mules for pack on Pack at Present. Proceeded with party to HAUTECLOCQUE. Two horses sold to Horse Butcher Bruay "D" cases	

Army Form C. 2118.

WAR DIARY
or
INTELLIGENCE SUMMARY.
(Erase heading not required.)

Instructions regarding War Diaries and Intelligence Summaries are contained in F. S. Regs., Part II. and the Staff Manual respectively. Title pages will be prepared in manuscript.

Place	Date 1919	Hour	Summary of Events and Information	Remarks and references to Appendices
LACOUVRIE	FEB 20		Inspected animals of 11th Corps Hy. Arty. Preparations made for sale on following day. A/A.D.V.S. visited and inspected all the animals. Animals admitted to Section for evacuation 16.	
"	21		Proceeded with the 50 animals to Trevent Sale. One pick class admitted to Section.	
"	22		Returned to Section. D.A.D.V.S. and D.A.D.V.S. visit. Evacuated 13 horses and 5 mules to V.E.S. Animals admitted 3.	
"	23		Visited Corps Field Cashier Paying in proceeds of Horse sale at Trevent.	
"	24		Visited D.A.D.V.S. office, and Field Cashier. Instructions received to move to H.Q. Loyinghem. Capt. Edwards supervising Section at La Beuvriere.	
"	25		Office Routine. Move to Loyinghem	

Army Form C. 2118.

WAR DIARY
or
INTELLIGENCE SUMMARY.

(Erase heading not required.)

Instructions regarding War Diaries and Intelligence Summaries are contained in F. S. Regs., Part II. and the Staff Manual respectively. Title pages will be prepared in manuscript.

Place	Date	Hour	Summary of Events and Information	Remarks and references to, Appendices
LAVENTIERE	FEB 1919 26		Admitted 4 cases for evacuation.	
"	27		Evacuated 5 animals to No. 11 V.E.S. Visited Rubrure and Huriorville with D.A.V.S. To inspect 200 animals and prepare for sale or Killers on March 1st	
"	28		Office Routine and preparation of forms and certificates for animals sold at Killem.	

J Oulsey Cap RAVC
O/c Mobile MVS

Major
D.A.D.V.S. 47th Div.

Army Form C. 2118.

LONDON MOBILE
VETERINARY SECTION
No. ....
Date MARCH 1919

WAR DIARY
or
INTELLIGENCE SUMMARY.
(Erase heading not required.)

Place	Date 1919	Hour	Summary of Events and Information	Remarks and references to Appendices
LOZINGHEM	MARCH 1		Sale of 199 Animals Blacs 2 Outfits at Lillers. Average prices obtained for Horses 800.50 francs. for Mules 639.50 francs. Gross amount realized 146,275 francs. One animal rejected from sale. Two animals admitted to Section for evacuation	
"	2		Office Routine. 4 Animals admitted to Section.	
"	3		Visited Field Cashier XI Corps, obtaining receipts & signature in respect of animal sale. Evacuated 6 animals to No. 11 V.E.S. Béthune.	
"	4		Office routine. One animal admitted to Section.	
"	5		Office routine.	
"	6		Inspected 200 Animals at Burbure, rejecting 9 marking for sale or killers. 3 Animals admitted to Section for evacuation.	

Army Form C. 2118.

1/2ND LONDON MOBILE VETERINARY SECTION
No. 1919
Date MARCH

WAR DIARY
or
INTELLIGENCE SUMMARY.
(Erase heading not required.)

Instructions regarding War Diaries and Intelligence Summaries are contained in F.S. Regs., Part II. and the Staff Manual respectively. Title pages will be prepared in manuscript.

Place	Date 1919	Hour	Summary of Events and Information	Remarks and references to Appendices
	MARCH			
LOZINGHEM	7		Office routine. One Horse admitted to Section. Four animals evacuated to No. 11. V.E.S. Bethune. One Horse destroyed, fractured Tibia.	
"	8		Sale of 199 Animals at Lillers. Gross amount realized 145,900 francs. Average price for Horses 794 francs, for mules 638 francs. One animal rejected unfit for sale. One Horse admitted to Section for evacuation. Money paid into Field Cashier XI Corps.	
"	9		Office routine.	
"	10		Visited Field Cashier XI Corps obtaining receipts & signatures in respect of sale at Lillers on the 8th. One Animal evacuated to No 11 V.E.S.	
"	11		Sale of 200 Horses & 76 59¾ Dun. at Bruay. Total amount realized 155,275 francs. Average price obtained for Horses 918.25 francs for mules 634.50 francs. Money paid into XI Corps Field Cashier. Three animals admitted to Section for evacuation.	

Army Form C. 2118.

WAR DIARY
or
INTELLIGENCE SUMMARY.
(Erase heading not required.)

1/2ND LONDON MOBILE VETERINARY SECTION
No. 1919
Date MARCH

Instructions regarding War Diaries and Intelligence Summaries are contained in F. S. Regs., Part II. and the Staff Manual respectively. Title pages will be prepared in manuscript.

Place	Date 1919	Hour	Summary of Events and Information	Remarks and references to Appendices
	MARCH			
LOZINGHEM	12		Section move to Chateau Monts Events. Two animals evacuated to No. 11. V.E.S. Office routine. Visits Field Butcher XI Corps obtaining receipts and signatures in respect of sale of animals at Enguin on 11th.	
"	13		Office routine. Two animals admitted for evacuation. Inspection at Bubure 200 animals for sale at Lillers on Saturday 15th.	
"	14		Office routine. One mule destroyed, buried, unfit for food.	
"	15		Sale of 199 Animals at Lillers. Gross amount realized 143,150 francs. Average prices obtained for horses 740 francs for Mules 668 francs. One animal rejected unfit for sale. Money paid in to XI Corps Field Cashier. One animal admitted to Section for evacuation.	
"	16		Office routine.	
"	17		Office routine. Visits Field Cashier XI Corps obtaining receipts and signatures in respect of sale of animals at Lillers on 15th.	

2353 Wt. W2514/1454 700,000 5/15 D. D. & L. A.D.S.S./Forms/C. 2118.

Army Form C. 2118.

1/2ND
LONDON MOBILE
VETERINARY SECTION
No......................
1919
Date. MARCH

WAR DIARY
or
INTELLIGENCE SUMMARY.
(Erase heading not required.)

Instructions regarding War Diaries and Intelligence Summaries are contained in F. S. Regs., Part II. and the Staff Manual respectively. Title pages will be prepared in manuscript.

Place	Date 1919	Hour	Summary of Events and Information	Remarks and references to Appendices
	MARCH			
LOZINGEM	18		Office routine. 2 Horses sold to Butcher at Bruay for 950 francs. Money paid to Field Cashier.	
"	19		Office routine.	
"	20		Visited BURBURE to inspect and mark animals for sale or Litter on the 22nd. One animal sold to Butcher at 475 francs. Money paid to Field Cashier. One animal admitted to Section for evacuation.	
"	21		Office routine.	
"	22		Sale of 291 Animals at Litter. Gross amount realized 257,945 francs average prices for Mules 819 francs for Horses 887 francs. Money paid into Field Cashier XI Corps.	
"	23		Office Routine.	

2353 Wt. W2514/1454 700,000 5/15 D. D. & L.   A.D.S.S./Forms/C. 2118.

Army Form C. 2118.

WAR DIARY
or
INTELLIGENCE SUMMARY.
(Erase heading not required.)

1/2ND LONDON MOBILE VETERINARY SECTION
No. ....
1919 MARCH

Instructions regarding War Diaries and Intelligence Summaries are contained in F. S. Regs. Part II. and the Staff Manual respectively. Title pages will be prepared in manuscript.

Place	Date 1919	Hour	Summary of Events and Information	Remarks and references to Appendices
	MARCH			
LOZINGHEM	24		Inspection and marking of 214 Animals at Bruay on 25th. Visited Field Cashier XI Corps obtaining receipts and signature in respect of sale at Lillers on 22nd.	
"	25		Sale of 221 Animals at Bruay. Gross total 180850 francs. Average prices obtained for horses 819 francs, for mules 781.25 francs. Money paid into Field Cashier XI Corps.	
	26		Office Routine	
	27		Office Routine	
	28		Visited XI Corps Field Cashier obtaining receipts in respect of Animal sale at Bruay on 25th. Proceeded on 14 days leave to U.K. prior to proceeding to Join X Corps Troops.	

Army Form C. 2118.

WAR DIARY
or
INTELLIGENCE SUMMARY.
(Erase heading not required.)

Instructions regarding War Diaries and Intelligence Summaries are contained in F. S. Regs., Part II. and the Staff Manual respectively. Title pages will be prepared in manuscript.

1/2ND LONDON MOBILE VETERINARY SECTION
No. ....
Date MARCH 1919

Place	Date 1919	Hour	Summary of Events and Information	Remarks and references to Appendices
LEZINGHEM	MARCH 29.		Office routine. Capt. J. MacBride takes over Mobile Section.	
	30		Office routine.	
	31		Office routine.	

W. Winter
Capt. R.A.V.C.
for O.C. 1/2 London M.V.S.

1/2ND LONDON MOBILE VETERINARY SECTION
No. WR/49
Date 4-4-19

CONFIDENTIAL.

47 F.R. Tra... O.S.B. 51

Army Form C. 2118.

WAR DIARY
or
INTELLIGENCE SUMMARY.
(Erase heading not required.)

Instructions regarding War Diaries and Intelligence Summaries are contained in F. S. Regs., Part II. and the Staff Manual respectively. Title pages will be prepared in manuscript.

Place	Date	Hour	Summary of Events and Information	Remarks and references to Appendices
CAMBRAIN CHATELAIN	May 1		Headquarters and Nos 1 & 2 Coys of F.R. Train at CAMBRAIN CHATELAIN. Rail head - BARLIN. 3 H.R.S. drawn and delivered to units by M.T. Ration strength - 17-26 Men. 83 Animals. 2/3 O.Rs. despatched on demobilization.	Ansd
			1/Lieut G.H. BOXALL proceeded to no 33rd Div. M.T. Coy for duty. Captain F.E. SALZMANN and 1/Lieut F. MOULTRAY proceeded Coy 1/C Army H.T. Reserve park for duty.	
			Jan 1/C Army H.T. Reserve park for duty. O/R Coys Waggons entrained at PERNES.	
	5		O.Rs. despatched on demobilization.	
			O/R Coy left PERNES for HOUCRE with T2 each of 140 Infantry Bde.	
			O/R Coy left for LANGUARD COMMON. 1/P.B.Oc RE 47 Machine Gun Bn. M.M.P. and R.A.O.D. transferred to 189 Bde RE 17 Corps for rations	
			O.K.T. Corps Troops for rations. Captain G.R. MANGATT reported to Headquarters, BETHUNE on & Non duty.	
	6		1/4 M.P.Bn R.W.F. vehicles arrived at PERNES with 78 mol force. 10 horses transferred to Brigs Animal Battering Camp, BARLIN.	
	7		H.Q. vehicles arrived at PERNES with H.Q. force.	
			Ration strength - 177 men 301 Boy chair vehicles entrained at PERNES. H.Q. 1/4 Bn R.W. Fang. 301 Boy chair vehicle transferred to Brigs Animal Bettering Camp, BARLIN.	
	9		Balance of Z. Oliv 10 horses transferred to Brigs Animal Bettering Camp, BARLIN.	